COINS AND MEDALS OF THE ENGLISH CIVIL WAR

COINS AND MEDALS OF THE ENGLISH CIVIL WAR

Second Edition

Edward Besly

Spink
In association with
Amgueddfa Cymru – National Museum Wales

First edition published in 1990 by B A Seaby Ltd
in association with The National Museum of Wales

This second edition published in 2019 and reprinted in 2026 by
Spink and Son Ltd in association with Amgueddfa Cymru – National Museum Wales

A CIP catalogue record for this book is available from the British Library.

ISBN 978-1-912667-01-7

Typeset by Russ Whittle
Printed in the UK on sustainably sourced paper by
4edge Limited, Hockley, Essex, SS5 4AD.

The Publisher's authorised representative in the EU for product safety is Authorised Rep Compliance Ltd., Ground Floor, 71 Lower Baggot Street, Dublin D02 P593, Ireland | www.arccompliance.com

Spink Books
An imprint of White Owl Collectables
George House, Units 13/14 Beevor Street
Barnsley, South Yorkshire S71 1HN
www.spinkbooks.com

CONTENTS

Preface to the Second Edition

Coins and Medals of the English Civil War was published in 1990. In 1992, an invitation to contribute to a series of lectures on Civil-War Exeter – marking the 350th anniversary of the war – acted as a spur to new research which produced a complete reappraisal of the mint there, its history and products. Further talks for regional meetings of the British Numismatic Society and the British Association of Numismatic Societies extended and refined my perspectives on many aspects of the subject; another invitation, in 2011, to revisit questions of hoards and hoarding allowed me to update work first published in 1987. The opportunity to publish a new edition is therefore most welcome: it includes many new coins and we meet more of the people who, willingly or unwillingly, did business with the mints of the Civil War.

In producing a new edition, I am indebted to the following for their permission to reproduce copyright images in their possession: The Ashmolean Museum, Oxford; Bristol Museum & Art Gallery; The British Library; Llyfrgell Genedlaethol Cymru/The National Library of Wales; The Trustees of the British Museum; the Claydon House Trust; Cornwall Record Office; The Rector and Scholars of Exeter College, Oxford; The Portable Antiquities Scheme; The Royal Mint Museum; The Society of Antiquaries of London; Wakefield Council; Sir Ferrers Vyvyan, Bt.

Unless otherwise indicated, the coins and medals illustrated are in the collection of the National Museum of Wales (Amgueddfa Cymru) and I am grateful to my colleagues James Wild, Kevin Thomas and Becky Brumbill for photography and digitisation; Tony Daly, for fig. 4.6 and Map 4; and Colin Williams, whose maps and other diagrams are reproduced from the first edition. All coins and medals are reproduced at their natural size. Particular thanks are also owed to Mark Stoyle, who shared so much information about Civil-War Exeter and Stephen Briggs, whose thoroughgoing mining of newly digitised newspaper archives has produced many new hoard records;

Philip Skingley, who suggested the production of this new edition; Emma Howard, who has brought it to fruition; and my colleagues who read the new text and offered helpful advice. Errors and omissions, as ever, are mine.

Dates and prices

At the time of the Civil War, England and Wales used the Old Style (Julian) calendar, which ran ten days behind the New Style (Gregorian), widely used on the Continent but not formally adopted in Britain until 1752, by which time the gap had increased to eleven days. The New Style year began on 1 January, but the English official year started on Lady Day, 25 March; English documents and coins (where they bore dates) produced between 1 January and 24 March inclusive bear the 'previous' year's date – 1 January 1642, for instance, *following* 31 December 1642. The receipt for Exeter College's plate (**3.7**) is a good example. Here, I have retained the Old Style days and months, as recorded by English contemporaries; years, however, are given in the New Style, starting on 1 January. The Venetian letters quoted in Chapter 3, originally dated New Style, have been aligned to the days and months used in England.

The monetary system of England and Wales was until 1971 based on the Pound (£) of twenty shillings (s), each of twelve pence (d). We retain the Pound, but in decimal form as 100 pence (p), its value severely eroded by inflation, notably during the later twentieth century. For Civil-War prices, especially of goods and services, the reader is referred to contemporary diaries and account-books, of which three Yorkshire examples and one from Exeter are given under *Further Reading*. Our present way of life is so different that formal comparison of the 'pound in the pocket' with that in the 1640s purse is not easy and this time has not been attempted.

Edward Besly
Penarth and Cardiff
August 2018

Chapter 1
PROLOGUE

Periods of conflict or uncertainty tend to yield numerous money hoards compared with times of peace and prosperity. Nowhere is this more true than of England and Wales during the Civil War, or 'Great Rebellion', in the reign of Charles I (1625-49). Thus, during the Stuart period, on average only about one-two hoards have been recorded for every year of the reigns of James I (1603-25), Charles II (1660-85) and even for the first dozen years of Charles I. But the decade 1639-49 has yielded (at the time of writing) more than 170 hoards that can be dated reasonably securely; and at least another 166 are likely to date from this period, but are only recorded vaguely in old newspaper reports and other traditions. For ordinary men and women, such wealth as they possessed consisted mainly of coins of the precious metals, silver and gold; there were no banks or building societies. So, when war broke out in 1642, many hid their cash in secure places, perhaps because they went off to fight, perhaps – increasingly as time passed – to avoid the exactions imposed by both sides. Death or enforced absence prevented many of them from recovering their money. Occasionally we hear about the recovery of such assets: late in 1645, the royalist Sir Henry Slingsby managed to collect £40 in gold from his home near York, then deep in enemy territory. Sometimes, others benefited: in 1658 repairs to Halton Castle, Cheshire, under Colonel Henry Brooke brought to light £506 hidden in the walls.

Today chance, usually with a little electronic assistance, continues to bring these caches to light and few years pass without the discovery in England and Wales of one or more 'Civil War hoards', such as the 152 coins buried in 1644-5, worth £7 1s 6d at the time, discovered during development work in Fore Street, Castle Cary, Somerset, in February 2006 (a spot I must have passed hundreds of times during the thirty-seven years my family lived in the town). Some hoards are substantial, for instance Ryhall, Rutland (face value £160 1s 0d; buried 1643, found in 1987) and the biggest of the lot, found at Middleham, Yorkshire in 1993: three pots containing 5,099 coins, in all worth around £313. The 30 gold and 1,552 silver coins (£93 5s 0d) found at Breckenbrough, North Yorkshire in June 1985 also provided evidence for local royalist provisioning in the form of receipts for cheese taken from two farms in January 1644. Wales, smaller and much poorer, has nevertheless produced at least 17 hoards, ranging from two substantial but ill-recorded finds from Conwy and Prestatyn in the north, through a hoard of 105 coins found at Penybryn Hall, near Wrexham in 1979 to the modest 35 silver coins found in the ruins of a *hafod* (seasonally-occupied upland farm building) near Pontypridd in south Wales in 1988. In 1996, the Welsh picture was sensationally enhanced by the discovery of 33 gold and 467 silver coins (£51 9s 0d: enough to pay 50 foot soldiers for a month, or to purchase two tons of cheese) at Tregwynt mansion, near Fishguard, North Pembrokeshire (**1.1**). A long-standing legend of buried treasure at the mansion, supposedly the result of local panic when the French landed at nearby Carreg Wastad point in February 1797 (the last time Britain was invaded by a foreign power), transpired to incorporate a somewhat earlier tradition!

Coins are therefore some of the commonest relics of this crucial and much-studied phase of British history. This book explores the coinage produced during the conflict and especially how the royalists, denied the mint at the Tower of London, set about producing their own coin of the realm. To set these issues in their monetary context we must first, though, examine the Tower coins already in circulation.

Coinage in early Stuart England and Wales

Almost all of the money circulating in England and Wales at the start of the Civil War had been produced at the Tower of London, which during the later Tudor and early Stuart periods housed the sole official mint; much of it had been produced many decades prior to 1642. The history of Eng-

Fig. 1.1 The Tregwynt hoard, North Pembrokeshire: the finest Civil War hoard yet found in Wales. The hoard is likely to have been concealed in 1648, the time of an important royalist/localist rebellion in the area. It was probably buried in a former outbuilding of Tregwynt mansion and came to light when the site was levelled for a tennis court in September 1996. *Site photo: E Besly*

lish coinage is characterized by long periods of stability in denominations, weight and alloy standards, even design, with occasional adjustments in response to changing bullion prices or a new reign. To judge from the hoards, the earliest silver coins still in regular circulation, apart from the occasional 'fine' groat of Henry VII or VIII, were those of good silver, introduced in 1551 to put an end to a decade of severe debasements under Henry VIII and Edward VI (**1.2**). Likewise, few gold coins dating from before Elizabeth I's reign were available for saving (Tregwynt included a Bristol crown of Henry VIII). 'Crown' gold (22 carats fine, or 916/1000), introduced in 1526, had become the norm. The old fine gold standard (23ct 3½ grains, or 99.5%) was retained only for the Angel (10s), struck under the Stuarts in minute quantities for the ceremony of 'touching for the King's Evil' (scrofula).

Fig. 1.2 Edward VI, silver sixpence, privy-mark *Tun*, 1551-3; Philip and Mary, silver groat (4d), p.m. *Fleur-de-lys*, 1554-8. Two of the earliest coins from the 1979 Penybryn (Ruabon, Wrexham) Treasure Trove, buried in 1644-5, showing the wear and tear resulting from ninety years or more of circulation.

Large discoveries of silver in Central Europe (the Tyrol, the Erzgebirge and in Saxony) from the later fifteenth century and in Spain's New World colonies during the sixteenth led to massive increases in the available amounts of precious metal, and one result was the production of the larger coins required for a rising level of international trade – and rising prices. Already in 1500, silver coins weighing up to one ounce (31g) were being struck by the silver-producing states in Austria and Germany as substitutes for gold coins of the same value. The new large coins caught on more slowly in other areas, especially on the fringes of Europe. In England the groat (fourpenny piece) had long been the largest silver coin. In 1504 Henry VII made an experimental issue of testoons, or shillings of twelve pence, but testoons did not become a regular part of the currency until the debasements of the 1540s. In 1560-1, when Elizabeth I caused the base monies of Henry VIII and Edward VI to be recoined, shillings were produced in large quantities as a matter of minting convenience. During much of the rest of her reign, the sixpence was the leading silver coin and these two denominations, with their equivalents produced under James I, often make up a large part of the value of hoards deposited during the Civil War (**1.3-1.5**).

Fig. 1.3 Elizabeth I, silver shilling, p.m. *One*, 1601; from the 1934 Prestatyn, Denbighshire, Treasure Trove, buried in 1643.

Fig. 1.4 Elizabeth I, silver sixpence, p.m. *Tun*, dated 1593. The rose behind the Queen's head and the added date served to distinguish the sixpence and its fractions (3d, 1½d, ¾d) from similar-sized coins of the groat series (4d, 2d, 1d) which were not so marked. *Prestatyn Treasure Trove*

Bigger silver coins still, half crowns (2s 6d) and crowns of five shillings, were first produced in 1551-3. Others were coined late in Elizabeth's reign and for James I, but quantities were small. Only during the 1630s did the silver half crown become an important coin in regular circulation, as a result of an arrangement whereby a proportion of the silver needed to pay Spain's troops in the Netherlands was from 1632 transported in English

Fig. 1.5 James I, silver shilling of 2nd coinage, p.m. Fleur-de-lys, 1604-5. The reverse legend 'Whom God hath joined, let no man put asunder' refers to the personal union of Scotland and England under James, who adopted the title 'King of Great Britain' in October 1604. *Prestatyn Treasure Trove*

ships, via Dover, taking advantage of England's neutrality in the European ('Thirty Years') war. At Dover, two-thirds of the silver was unloaded and sent to the Tower Mint, where Spanish agents paid the necessary charges and then used the recoined silver to buy bills of exchange redeemable in Flanders. The remaining third (increased to two-thirds in 1638) was re-exported directly, against a duty of 1½ per cent. The result was a dramatic increase both in the Mint's output of silver (a mere £143,000 in the six years 1626-32 became nearly £4 million, or about 475 tons of silver coins, in the decade 1632-42) and in the amount of silver circulating in England and Wales, coupled with a massive drain of gold to the Continent as debts were settled there using the higher value metal, which was much less bulky to transport. As a correspondent noted in 1652, 'we have in Amsterdam more English gold than you yourselves have in all England, this gold hath been all sent within twenty years…' and this is echoed both in the Civil War hoards, the vast majority of which consist solely of silver coins, or at most contain one or two of gold, and the frequency with which weights for English gold appear in the sets used by Flemish merchants to check those most commonly passing through their hands (**1.6-1.8**).

Fig. 1.6 James I, gold Unite of twenty shillings, 2nd coinage, p.m. *Key*, 1609-10. The name 'Unite' was ordained by proclamation, 16 November 1604. The rising price of gold relative to silver forced the Unite to be raised to 22s in 1612 and by 1661 it was valued at 23s 6d. *Tregwynt Treasure Trove*

Fig. 1.7 James I, gold twenty shillings, or 'Laurel', 3rd coinage, p.m. *Spur Rowe*l, 1619-20. New, lighter gold coins proclaimed on 31 July 1619 remedied the 'perplexities in reckoning' occasioned by the 1612 revaluation and restored gold coins of 5s, 10s and 20s, 'stamped on the one side with Our picture crowned with a laurell' – and with their values. *Tregwynt Treasure Trove*

Fig. 1.8 Charles I, gold twenty shillings, p.m. *Fleur-de-lys*, 1625. Charles's gold continued the standards of James I's third ('laurel') coinage. *Tregwynt Treasure Trove*

Fig. 1.9 Charles I, silver half crown, p.m. *Crown*, 1635-7. The reverse legend, 'I reign by Christ's favour', alludes to Charles's belief in the divine right of Kings and appears on the four largest silver types (5s, 2s 6d, 1s, 6d). *Penybryn Treasure Trove*

Fig. 1.10 Charles I, silver penny, p.m. *Fleur-de-lys*, 1625-6. Later Tower Mint pence bore the King's portrait and the royal arms.

Of the coins for everyday use at the lower end of the scale, only groats are found in any quantity in hoards, though silver pieces down to the unmanageably small silver halfpenny are sometimes encountered. Pence (**1.10**) and half groats are frequently found on their own, representing casual losses. Official coinage in copper had yet to be developed, but the City of Bristol had issued square copper farthing tokens under licence from the Crown in Elizabeth's reign. Royal copper-alloy farthing tokens, first authorized in 1613, were made under licence by a sequence of noble contractors, ostensibly to ease small transactions and to aid poor relief, in practice for their own profit. Successive patentees refused to redeem those issued by their predecessors; in 1634 John Hayne in Exeter had to sell thirty shillings in 'old farthings' at a massive discount, receiving only ten shillings for them.

Fig. 1.11 Copper farthing token in the name of Charles I. 'Rose' type, produced under licence from 1636 by Lord Maltravers and Sir Francis Crane.

The farthing tokens are found today in large numbers (**1.11**); they were frequently counterfeited (despite heavy penalties which included fines, the pillory and imprisonment) and were alleged to have been produced by the royalists in Bristol during the Civil War.

In their designs, the Tudor coinages retained some vestiges of the uniform medieval types, notably in using a cross as the basic element of the reverse. However, portraits had become naturalistic (**1.3**) and other modernizing features, such as Roman lettering, coats of arms, statements of value, even the date (**1.4**) had all appeared by 1600. From Elizabeth I onwards, we may note also the left and right alternation of the royal portraits, which to the present day remains a feature of British coinage (e.g., **1.3**, **1.5**, **1.9**). Although the basic designs and legends were prescribed, they could be treated in many different ways, depending on the engraver. We shall see this, for instance, in the equestrian effigies on the crowns and half crowns, some of which were anything but realistic.

Fig. 1.12 Scotland, James VI, gold sword-and-sceptre piece (£6 Scottish), Eighth coinage, Edinburgh 1602. Proclaimed legal tender in England and Wales in 1603, at ten shillings. *Tregwynt Treasure Trove*

Fig. 1.13 Scotland, James VI, silver thistle merk (13s 4d Scottish), Eighth coinage, Edinburgh 1602. Legal tender in England and Wales from 1603 at 13½d, together with its fractions: half-, quarter- and eighth-merks.

The circulating medium was completed by small quantities of coins from other countries, such as the Scottish gold (**1.12**) and silver (**1.13**) brought to London by James VI and I and his retinue following his English accession and promptly declared legal tender in England and Wales by proclamation, on 8 April 1603; and the shillings and sixpences struck at the Tower Mint between 1603 and 1607 for use in Ireland (**1.14**). The silver types, unfamiliar in design and awkwardly valued, seem to have been coins that people were happy to be rid of – part of the Ship Money tax collected in Monmouthshire in 1639 was described by the Sheriff as 'such ragged pieces as broken groats, quarter pieces of thirteen pence halfpennies, ten pence halfpennies [*what were they?*], harpers and fourpence halfpennies ... the which I intend, God willing, to change into good money or gold'. Post-Union Scottish coins, of both James VI and Charles I, were the exact equivalents of their English counterparts in weights, standards and general designs, mingling happily into English circulation at an exchange rate of 12 shillings Scots to one shilling English (e.g., **1.15**).

Fig. 1.14 James I, shilling for Ireland, London, p.m. *Martlet*, 1604-5. Legal tender in England and Wales at ninepence, being of sterling silver but only three-quarters the weight of its English counterpart. The Irish sixpence was also current, at 4½d.

Fig. 1.15 Scotland, James VI, Post-Union silver thirty shillings, equivalent to an English half crown. *Tregwynt Treasure Trove*

From time to time it was deemed expedient to allow certain Continental types to circulate in England and Wales. Foreign gold coins, such as French and Burgundian crowns, were officially allowed under Elizabeth; other types were tolerated unofficially. Royal marriages also played a part: in 1554 Mary Tudor made a range of Spanish gold and silver coins legal tender at valuation, based on 1 real = 6½d, and although Elizabeth I promptly banned it, Spanish silver seems to have been tolerated in England into the seventeenth century. In 1613 James I forbade the use of clipped Spanish silver, which disrupted the 'benefit previously brought to trade' by the use of Spanish coins of full weight. Nevertheless, heavily-worn silver reals and half-reals of the sixteenth century appear from time to time in hoards of the Civil War years.

The dowry brought by Henrietta Maria on her marriage to Charles in 1625 included 'good summes of money of the coyne of France', recoinage of which was frustrated by an outbreak of the plague in London, which closed the Mint. Accordingly, the silver 'cardecue' (quart d'écu) was proclaimed legal tender at nineteen pence halfpenny on 4 September 1625 (**1.16**). Importing of light cardecues was strictly forbidden, but proved impossible to control. On 6 July 1626, for instance, the Mayor of Newcastle reported to the Privy Council that in May searchers had confiscated 2,178 cardecues which French merchants had used to buy coal. They were generally found to be light and not worth above 16d. Shortly afterwards, on 24 July, the cardecue was demonetized, though its use lingered on a little while. On 2 January 1627, one Stephen Morrell of Colne deposed that he had been robbed at Preston fair on 28 October 1626 of a purse containing 46 shillings, three 'cartdekues' and a broken shilling.

Coin Manufacture

The production of coinage was strictly controlled by contract between the Crown and the Master-Worker(s) of the Mint. Bullion brought to the Mint

Fig. 1.16 France, Henri IV (1589-1610), silver quart d'écu or 'cardecue', Bayonne mint (identified by the letter L below the reverse shield), 1598. Legal tender in England and Wales at 19½d, 1625-6. (See also 7.1).

Fig. 1.17 The surviving portion of the 1601 silver trial plate, which bears the impression of the reverse of a sixpence of that year. *Crown Copyright; image supplied by the Royal Mint Museum*

was purchased at a set price, turned into coinage of specified denominations with weights and alloy standards fixed within narrow limits (see Table I), and reissued subject to defined charges to cover minting costs and profits and the King's 'royalty' or seigniorage. By way of safeguard, samples were withdrawn at random from every 'journey' of coins (30 lb in the case of silver) and sealed in a box for regular, roughly annual, 'trials of the Pyx' at which weight and fineness were tried by a jury drawn from the London Goldsmiths' Company, against samples taken from standard plates of the prescribed composition (**1.17**). To this end all of the dies were given a privy-mark, a private symbol sometimes described today as a mint- or initial- mark, which also enables us to date the coins, since before 1649 only a minority of English coins incorporated an explicit date in their designs. This mark – a harp, a crown, a scallop-shell (the coins illustrated and Table II, of Charles I's marks, give an idea of the variety of choices) – was appended at the Master-Worker's orders in accordance with his indenture with the Crown: 'he … shall be holden and bound to make a privy mark to all the moneys that shall be made by him so that if need should be he may know and discern which moneys … amongst others be made by him and which not …' as Thomas Bushell's 1637 indenture for the Aberystwyth mint puts it.

Table I: *The English Monetary System of Charles I, 1625-42*

GOLD (Tower Mint only)	SILVER
22 ct fine (91.6%)	*11 oz 2 dwt fine* (92.5%)
Twenty shillings, 41 to the Troy pound	Five shillings, or Crown (Tower only)
Ten shillings	Two shillings and sixpence, or Half Crown
Five shillings	Shilling, 62 to the Troy pound*
	Sixpence
23 ct 3½ gr fine (99.5%)	Fourpence, or Groat (Aberystwyth only)
Ten shillings (Angel), 89 to the Troy pound (for ceremonial use)	Threepence (Aberystwyth only)
	Twopence
	Penny
	Halfpenny

Notes:

One pound (£) = twenty shillings, each of twelve pence (d)

One Troy pound weight = twelve ounces

One Troy ounce = 20 pennyweights = 480 grains = 31.10 grammes

One gramme = 15.43 grains

* On 14 August 1626, the weight of silver coins was reduced to 70s 6d to the Troy pound but this debasement was short-lived, the standard reverting to 62s on 8 November.

Table II: *Tower Mint privy-marks and pyx trials of Charles I from 1625 until 1643*

	Lys	29 June 1626
	Cross on steps	27 April 1627
	Negro head	27 April 1627
	Castle	3 July 1628
	1st Anchor	6 June 1629
	Heart	23 June 1630
	Feathers	30 June 1631
	Rose	21 June 1632
	Harp	11 July 1633
	Portcullis	27 June 1634
	Bell	18 June 1635
	Crown	14 February 1637
	Tun	8 May 1638
	2nd Anchor	4 July 1639
	Triangle	26 July 1640
	Star	15 July 1641
	Triangle-in-circle	29 May 1643

The control of weight and fineness was of great importance for both gold and silver, since the face values of the coins were closely related to the intrinsic value of their metal, unlike our own today, which are simply tokens. For silver the fineness, which was measured in terms of the Troy (twelve-ounce) pound weight of finished metal, was set at 11 ounces and 2 pennyweights, with 18 dwt of 'alloy' – in modern terms 92.5% of pure metal, or sterling silver; gold coins for circulation were 22 carats (91.6%) fine. Because precision was hard to achieve, a variation, the 'remedy', was allowed both in weight and fineness, of two pennyweights in the pound (0.833%) either side of the standard.

Fig. 1.18 Minting, purportedly at the Tower of London, depicted by Holinshed (1577). The activities shown here – weighing of bullion and the cutting, annealing (or blanching), hammering and coining of the blanks were in practice carried out in separate workshops. On the extreme right coins are produced by hammering blanks between two iron dies. The woman working at the front left reminds us that moneying was very much a 'family business'. *British Library 598.h.4*

Tudor and early Stuart coinage stands at the end of a long tradition of production by manual methods. The sequence of operations, some of which are shown in **1.18**, was long and complicated. Bullion was first melted, assayed and adjusted to the correct fineness and then cast into thin ingots, which were reduced to the required thickness by a sequence of beatings and annealings; blanks were cut and further annealed, then stacked and hammered into an approximately circular shape. After more annealing they were blanched by boiling in an acid solution ('argol' – potassium tartrate from the lees of wine) and turned into coin by hammering between two engraved dies. The dies themselves were made of iron with steeled faces (**1.19**). Designs were 'engraved' on their faces using small positive punches, a technique used since Anglo-Saxon times; by now larger elements such as the King's head were formed from single punches, giving the coinage a certain uniformity of appearance. The lower die, or pile, bore a spike by which it was anchored in a bench or block and was the die which bore the King's portrait; the upper die, or trussel, was hand held and received direct hammer blows. It therefore wore out faster than the other, two or more trussels being needed for every pile that was made. In 1639-40 two workers, Thomas Mason and Richard Martin, made a total of 3,904 coinage irons: 60 for gold coins (20 piles, 40 trussels) and 3,844 for silver (1,236 piles and 2,608 trussels). We do not know how many of these became finished dies, but the silver output that year (over £400,000: some millions of coins) dwarfed that of gold (£39,000).

The sixteenth and seventeenth centuries saw a gradual transition in Europe to the use of machinery for some of these operations: rolling mills for ingots, punches to cut out the blanks, devices for marking their edges, and the coining operation itself. These changes were prompted by aesthetic considerations, desire for improved efficiency, the technical problems of handling the increased amounts of precious metal reaching the mints, and the need to combat the twin menaces of clipping and counterfeiting.

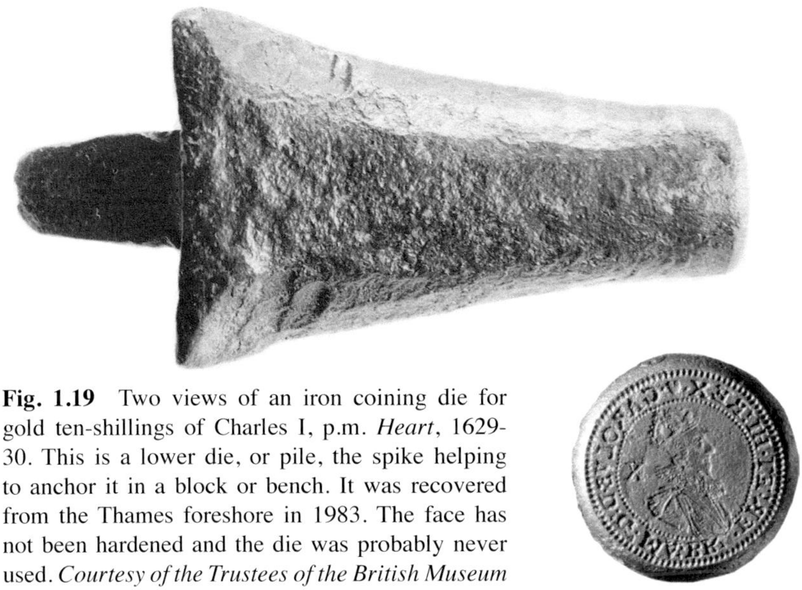

Fig. 1.19 Two views of an iron coining die for gold ten-shillings of Charles I, p.m. *Heart*, 1629-30. This is a lower die, or pile, the spike helping to anchor it in a block or bench. It was recovered from the Thames foreshore in 1983. The face has not been hardened and the die was probably never used. *Courtesy of the Trustees of the British Museum*

The appearance of the finished coin was above all determined by the skill of the moneyers. The new large silver denominations of the sixteenth century were hard to strike satisfactorily by traditional methods, even though devices such as drop-hammers may have been used to increase the available power. Machines devised for the coining process used one of two methods, percussive striking or something akin to rotary printing. The former, which ultimately became universal, employed dies mounted in a screw press. The latter was essentially a modification of the rolling mill, whereby groups of dies were engraved on steel rollers (in German *Walzen*, hence *Walzenprägung*), and the coins formed by passing strips of metal between them. Some of the larger European mints, for instance Hall in the Tyrol and Segovia in Spain, harnessed water power to drive both rolling mills and coining machines, though they could – up to a point – be worked by hand, since the designs were imprinted progressively as the strip passed through and less instantaneous force was required. Finished coins were punched out in a separate operation and, at Hall, tumbled in sand to remove rough edges. The method produced a much higher proportion of waste ('scissel') than the older methods. A variant of the rotary method, perhaps developed in response to practical problems encountered with the 'roller' method, involved the use of a simple hand-operated machine. Here, single pairs of dies with curved surfaces were mounted in pockets (German *Taschen* → *Taschenwerk*) on two parallel axles. Prepared blanks were fed between them to produce coins. In English, this type of machine is usually called a rocker press, which refers to the to-and-fro motion of the dies.

These mechanical innovations had largely passed England by (**1.20**). The only serious experiments with coining machines at the Tower Mint were made by two Frenchmen, Eloi Mestrelle and Nicholas Briot. From 1561 to 1572, Mestrelle produced small quantities of 'milled' coin for Elizabeth I, probably using a simple screw press (**1.21**). Rotary methods were known in London by the end of the century, but found use only in experiments for small change and in medal-making. In 1613, however, the newly-licensed royal farthing tokens were made 'exactly and artificially of copper, by Engins and instruments', using cylindrical 'roller' dies.

Fig. 1.20 Charles I, Tower shilling, p.m. *Heart*, 1629-30, with 'feathers' on the reverse denoting the use of Welsh silver at the Mint. A characteristic hammer-struck coin showing slight doubling of parts of the legends as a result of repeated blows.

Fig. 1.21 Elizabeth I, shilling, p.m. *Star*, 1561-2, milled issue. Mestrelle's precise technique is not known, but he seems to have used a form of screw press.

Fig. 1.22 Charles I, silver crown by Nicholas Briot, p.m. *Flower*, 1631-2. A beautiful example of Briot's abilities as engraver and engineer, produced using a rotary (rocker) press.

Fig. 1.23 Scotland, Charles I, thirty shillings, Edinburgh 1637-42. Sir John Falconer's issue, using a Briot rocker press. Perfection was less easily obtained in a routine production run, as can be seen by comparison with 1.22.

In 1625 Briot, engraver-general of the Paris Mint, fell out with his masters and came to London. He was welcomed by Charles I and thereafter engraved most of the effigies for the Tower coinage. He also produced experimental issues of coins using rotary methods, in 1631-2 and 1638-9, but was dogged by teething troubles, notably in controlling the weights of individual coins. Like Mestrelle before him, he failed to persuade the mint authorities to adopt his methods, despite the superior appearance of his products (**1.22**). Briot's work was also slow, and the need to coin large amounts of silver rapidly in the years after 1632 may explain their reluctance to pursue this form of manufacture. However, in 1635 Briot was appointed Master of the Scottish mint and from 1637 was allowed to install and use his machinery at Edinburgh (**1.23**). When civil war threatened in 1642 Briot, by now back in London, and his assistant David Ramage prepared equipment for two proposed royalist mints at Shrewsbury and York. The latter, as we shall see, used rotary methods, as did several other royalist mints in the Welsh Marches. Following further experiments under the Commonwealth and Protectorate, mechanized production was finally adopted at the Tower mint in 1663 using screw presses, by now proven to be the superior technique. This survey of England's Civil War coinage thus neatly encompasses the halting progress of the country's coinage manufacture into the machine age.

Thomas Bushell, Welsh Silver and the Aberystwyth Mint

From a hesitant start under Elizabeth, but more consistently from 1623, late in James I's reign, small quantities of silver from the Mines Royal in Cardiganshire, refined from argentiferous lead on the spot, were shipped regularly to London to be coined at the Tower Mint. To publicize the Welsh mines, the coins were marked on the reverse, above the royal arms, with the feathers badge of the Prince of Wales (**1.24**), though in practice the highly-refined Welsh metal was melted together with other consignments to bring them up to the mint standard. Coins bearing the feathers were produced until 1638 (**1.25**) and from 1627 until 1632 Wales was the source of almost all of the small amounts of silver coined in London, about £23,000 (**1.20**).

Fig. 1.24 James I, half crown, p.m. *Thistle*, 1621-3; one of the first coins to bear the 'Welsh feathers'. From the Bridgewater House collection, formed in the later part of the seventeenth century.

Fig. 1.25 Charles I, crown, p.m. Tun, 1637-8, the last mark to include Welsh silver struck in London in his reign. From the collection of Dr John Sharp, Archbishop of York (1645-1714).

Fig. 1.26 Thomas Bushell, future Aberystwyth mint master, aged about 30. A woodcut from his The First Part of Youth's Errors, 1628. *British Library 851.f.38*

Thomas Bushell (**1.26**) was born to a minor Worcestershire gentry family at Cleeve Prior, in the Vale of Evesham, late in Elizabeth I's reign. As a young man during James I's time he was in the service of Sir Francis Bacon and stayed with him until Bacon's death in 1626. After a spell of eremitical solitude on the Calf of Man, he returned to London, where he made a comfortable living from the likes of the farm of duties on silk-dyeing and a share of the soap-monopoly – and a remarkable ability to survive on credit: he was memorably described by John Aubrey as 'the greatest arts-master of running in debt (perhaps) in the world'; in today's parlance, certainly one to 'max out' his credit card.

In 1636 Bushell bought the lease of the Cardiganshire Mines Royal and set about improving them using up-to-date drainage and mining techniques. He petitioned to have a mint set up locally, in Aberystwyth Castle (**1.27**) and on 30 July 1637 was empowered to proceed by letters patent in the form of an indenture between the King and himself. Repairs to the castle and the setting-up of the mint were followed by the first delivery of silver ingots to the moneyers on 18 January 1639. Procedures were similar to those of the Tower Mint, except that all of the dies were engraved in London and supplied ready for use; the coins themselves and the low proportion of scissel recorded confirm traditional 'hammered' techniques. The mint had its own officers and a team of three moneyers on secondment from the Tower, Bushell himself combining the posts of Warden and Master-Worker. Other labour was recruited locally.

Fig. 1.27 Bushell's mint at Aberystwyth Castle, Ceredigion. *National Museum of Wales*

Fig. 1.28 Aberystwyth, half crown, *c*.1642. Its obverse die was amongst those taken to Shrewsbury by Bushell late in September that year.

Fig. 1.29 Aberystwyth, shilling and groat, p.m. *Open book*, 1639-42.

Bushell's indenture provided for the production of five of the same denominations as the Tower Mint: half crowns (**1.28**), shillings, sixpences, half groats and pence, but not crowns or halfpence. A supplementary commission dated 22 February 1638 added the halfpenny, as well as groats and threepences – a notable departure, perhaps intended to remedy the poor state of those already in circulation (**1.29**); no groats had been coined since 1561 and no threepences since 1582. Certainly, these two denominations are the commonest Aberystwyth products surviving today. By Bushell's express wish, the feathers appeared on *both* sides, except the three smallest coins, where they formed the main feature of the reverse (**1.30**); he chose as his privy-mark an open book, perhaps to denote that this new departure in providing coinage had nothing to conceal, unlike so many Stuart monopolies. In a little over three and a half years, the Aberystwyth mint produced around £10,500 in silver coin; it has been the subject of a comprehensive study by George C. Boon (1981: see *Further Reading*).

Fig. 1.30 Aberystwyth, smaller coins: half groat, penny, halfpenny, with Welsh feathers prominent as reverse design.

Chapter 2

CIVIL WAR

In the summer of 1642, England went to war with herself. The origins of this war and the political manoeuvrings of the 1640s have been much discussed elsewhere and are best described by the historian (see *Further Reading*). The purpose of this chapter is twofold: to give a very brief summary of the main events of the war; and to survey royalist minting in its geographical and operational context, as an introduction to the chapters that follow.

The Progress of the War, 1642-6 (see Map 1)

Charles I left London on 10 January 1642 and in March established his court at York. In May he sent for the Great Seal, which was conveyed secretly to the King by its Keeper, Lord Lyttleton. War looked certain, though Charles was frustrated in his bid for arms stored at Hull, and broke out formally on 22 August, when the King raised his standard at Nottingham and proceeded to Shrewsbury to recruit in Wales and the Marches. Both sides tried to secure the local militias and their arms. It was generally expected that a single campaign would settle matters, but the first major battle, at Edgehill on 23 October, was inconclusive. The royalists advanced on London, sacked Brentford on 12 November, but were then turned back by the capital's trained bands drawn up at Turnham Green. Charles established his wartime capital at Oxford.

1643 saw important royalist successes, notably the conquest of most of the West Country and the capture of Bristol. The Marquess of Newcastle, having finally overrun all of Yorkshire (except Hull) advanced into Lincolnshire, but his reluctance to move further afield cost the King his only opportunity to make inroads into East Anglia, where an anti-parliamentarian rising at Kings Lynn (July-August) finally withered for lack of royalist support. Inability to combine their various armies in a concerted campaign frustrated the royalist advance on London, which was halted by the drawn first battle of Newbury (20 September). Meanwhile parliamentarian strongholds such as Plymouth, Lyme Regis and especially Gloucester tied down forces and always threatened the royalist rear; the siege of Gloucester was relieved by the Earl of Essex on 5 September.

In attempting to force a solution, both sides sought help from outside, the King from Ireland, where an English army was countering the rebellion which had broken out in 1641, and Parliament, at great expense, from the Scots. An Anglo-Irish force of about 3,000 men arrived in north-east Wales late in November 1643, relieving pressure on the royalist garrison of Chester and taking part in several successful skirmishes, before being routed by Sir Thomas Fairfax and Sir William Brereton at Nantwich on 25 January 1644.The arrival of the Scots, however, was to prove one of the decisive factors that swung the war towards Parliament.

In 1644, although their western army was halted at Alresford in Hampshire on 29 March, the King's forces held their own in the south. One parliamentarian force was worsted at Cropredy, north of Oxford (6 June) and the invasion of the West by the Earl of Essex ended in disaster when the King trapped his army in Cornwall, though the investment of Taunton once again forced the royalists to waste men, materials and time in an unsuccessful siege. A second battle at Newbury (27 October) was again inconclusive.

In the north, however, a major royalist defeat at Selby (11 April) was followed by the arrival of the Scots and the siege of York. Prince Rupert, the King's nephew, after relieving Newark and conducting a lightning campaign in Lancashire, outwitted the besieging armies and relieved York on 1 July; the following day, however, his army was shattered at Marston Moor, the largest set-piece engagement of the war. The royalists thereby lost the entire north of England. The winter saw a thorough overhaul of parliamentarian forces, with the creation of the New Model Army and its consequences: Sir Thomas Fairfax became Commander-in-Chief, with Oliver Cromwell as commander of the horse. Peace negotiations at Uxbridge came to nothing.

Map 1 England and Wales during the Civil War, showing locations mentioned in the text

Despite losing Shrewsbury on 22 February, the 1645 campaign seemed to start well for the royalists. But on 30-31 May Prince Rupert stormed and sacked Leicester, provoking a parliamentarian response which led directly to the battle of Naseby on 14 June (**2.1**). Here the King's field army was destroyed and his baggage and secret correspondence captured. The battle of Langport (10 July) and the fall of Bristol on 11 September opened the way to the West Country. The King continued to hope for help from out-

Fig. 2.1 The order of battle at Naseby, 14 June 1645 (detail), from Joshua Sprigge, *Anglia Rediviva*, London 1647. Note the parliamentarian Forlorn Hope of musketeers. *National Museum of Wales Library*

side, but mishandled negotiations with the Irish Catholics proved a great embarrassment, while the Marquess of Montrose's brilliant campaign in Scotland came to an end when he was beaten at Philiphaugh, south of Edinburgh, on 13 September. Mopping-up operations in England lasted well into 1646, Pendennis in Cornwall being the last garrison to surrender, on 17 August. In Wales, Harlech held out until 13 March 1647. The King himself had slipped out of his besieged capital and surrendered himself to the Scots army near Newark on 5 May 1646.

At first, most of the money required to clothe, feed, equip and above all to pay the King's army was raised in cash from his supporters as gifts or as loans at the standard rate of eight per cent *per annum*, or was seized from opponents. The King may have had an advantage over his adversaries here, since many of the wealthiest men supported him, notably the Marquess of Worcester at Raglan Castle and his heir Edward, Lord Herbert. There are also records of substantial loans from many individuals: the architect Inigo Jones proffered £500, Sir Thomas Gower £1,500 and so on. The universities of Oxford and Cambridge played their part: in early July Dr Richard Chaworth was sent from York to borrow money from Oxford University. Exeter College sent £300 (**2.2**), All Souls £650. Both had to borrow heavily – the frequently-repeated comment that the universities sent plate at this juncture may be somewhat misleading, for it is evident that many of the Oxford colleges only yielded their plate the following January. By 20 July, about £10,000 had reached the King from Oxford.

With a short campaign in prospect, rates of pay could be generous and will have tempted those whose normal wages were only a few pence per day. The royalist Earl of Northampton offered as much as two shillings (24d) per day to raise a private army to besiege Warwick Castle; its parliamentarian owner, Lord Brooke, paid his garrison 4s 8d per man per week (i.e., 8d per day). The latter rate was also offered by royalist recruiters at Myddle, in Shropshire, and seems to have become the standard rate for infantry, on

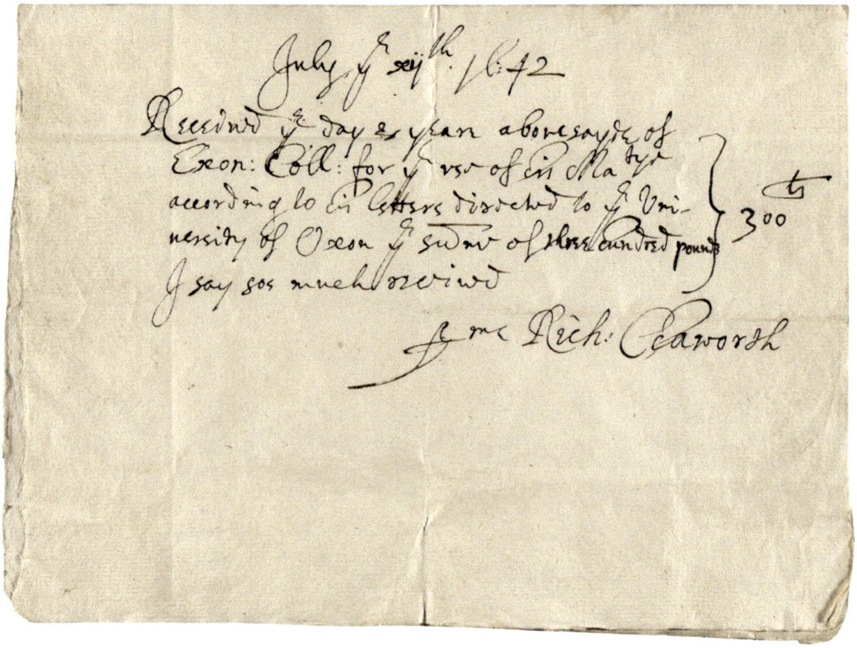
July ye xijth 1642
Received ye day & year aforesayde of Exon: Coll: for ye use of his Matye according to his letters directed to ye University of Oxon ye summe of three hundred pounds } £300
I say soe much received
p me Rich: Chaworth

Fig. 2.2 Royalist fund-raising, 12 July 1642: a receipt signed by Dr Richard Chaworth, MP for Midhurst and Chancellor of the diocese of London, for £300 contributed by Exeter College, Oxford, in response to the King's appeal to the University; £138 of this had to be borrowed (see p.45). By 20 July, £10,000 from Oxford University had reached the King at York. *Exeter College Archives, Charles I correspondence; published with permission of the Rector and Scholars of Exeter College, Oxford.*

both sides. Early in September 1642 (**2.3**), Sir John Byron offered a better rate for foot (6s per week), but his basic pay of 1s 6d per day for dragoons and 2s 6d for cavalry (who had to provide their own horses) matches exactly the rates for these categories in the parliamentarian Eastern Association in 1644-5. In royalist York, the trained bands (local militia) were paid twenty pence (1s 8d) per man per week.

Much of the country's portable wealth was in the form of silver plate (manufactured vessels, dishes, etc); this too was donated or 'lent'. A Receiver of Plate, Dr Stephen Goffe, was appointed at York on 3 August 1642, empow-

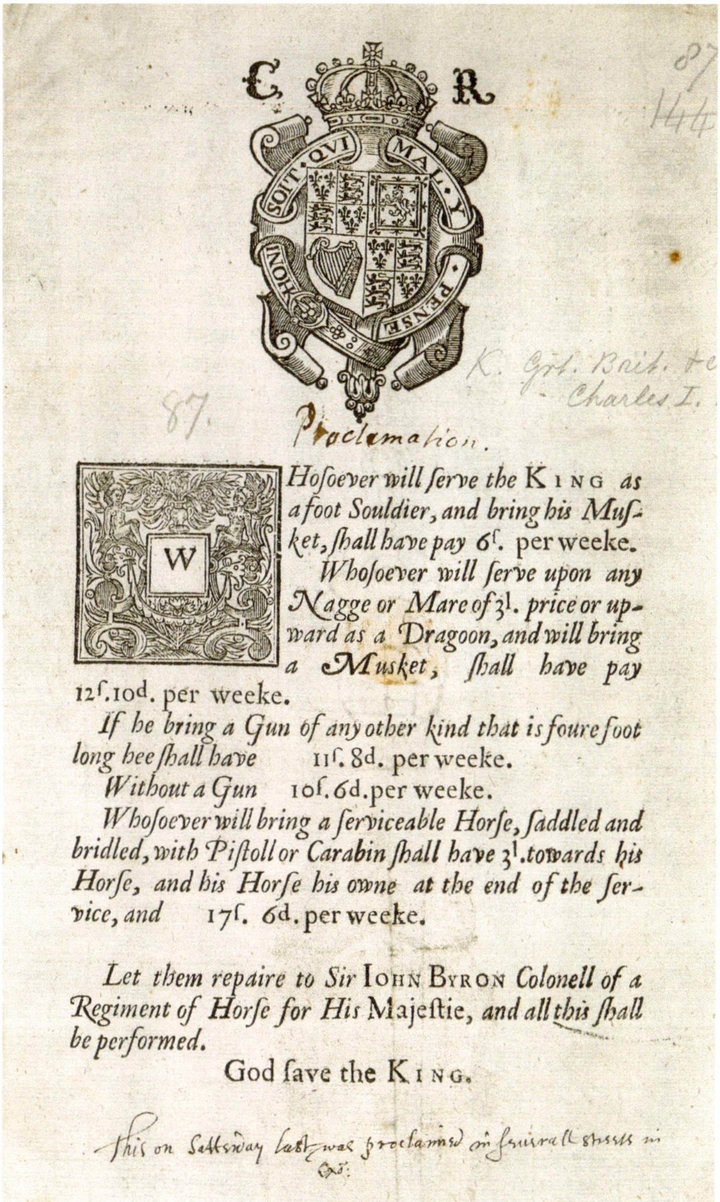
C R

HONI SOIT QUI MAL Y PENSE

Proclamation.

WHoſoever will ſerve the KING as a foot Souldier, and bring his Muſket, ſhall have pay 6ſ. per weeke.

Whoſoever will ſerve upon any Nagge or Mare of 3l. price or upward as a Dragoon, and will bring a Musket, ſhall have pay 12ſ.10d. per weeke.

If he bring a Gun of any other kind that is foure foot long hee ſhall have 11ſ. 8d. per weeke.

Without a Gun 10ſ. 6d. per weeke.

Whoſoever will bring a ſerviceable Horſe, ſaddled and bridled, with Piſtoll or Carabin ſhall have 3l. towards his Horſe, and his Horſe his owne at the end of the ſervice, and 17ſ. 6d. per weeke.

Let them repaire to Sir IOHN BYRON Colonell of a Regiment of Horſe for His Majeſtie, and all this ſhall be performed.

God ſave the KING.

This on Satterday last was proclaimed in severall streets in Ox:

Fig. 2.3 A royalist recruiting poster, displayed at Oxford. Sir John (later Lord) Byron was colonel of the first regiment of horse raised for the King and occupied the city from 28 August until 10 September. Note the high rates of pay and the appeal for equipment; the annotation indicates that the poster was put up on Saturday 3 September. *British Library 21.h.1 (87)*

ered to collect and give receipts for money or plate given or tendered for the King's service. Other sources of bullion included foreign coin (notably from the Low Countries, where the Queen worked tirelessly to raise loans), personal jewellery, prize-goods, and newly-mined Welsh silver, the last of which provided the royalists with a steady income of around £100 per week. Displaced from London, the royalists needed mints to convert these contributions into negotiable coin.

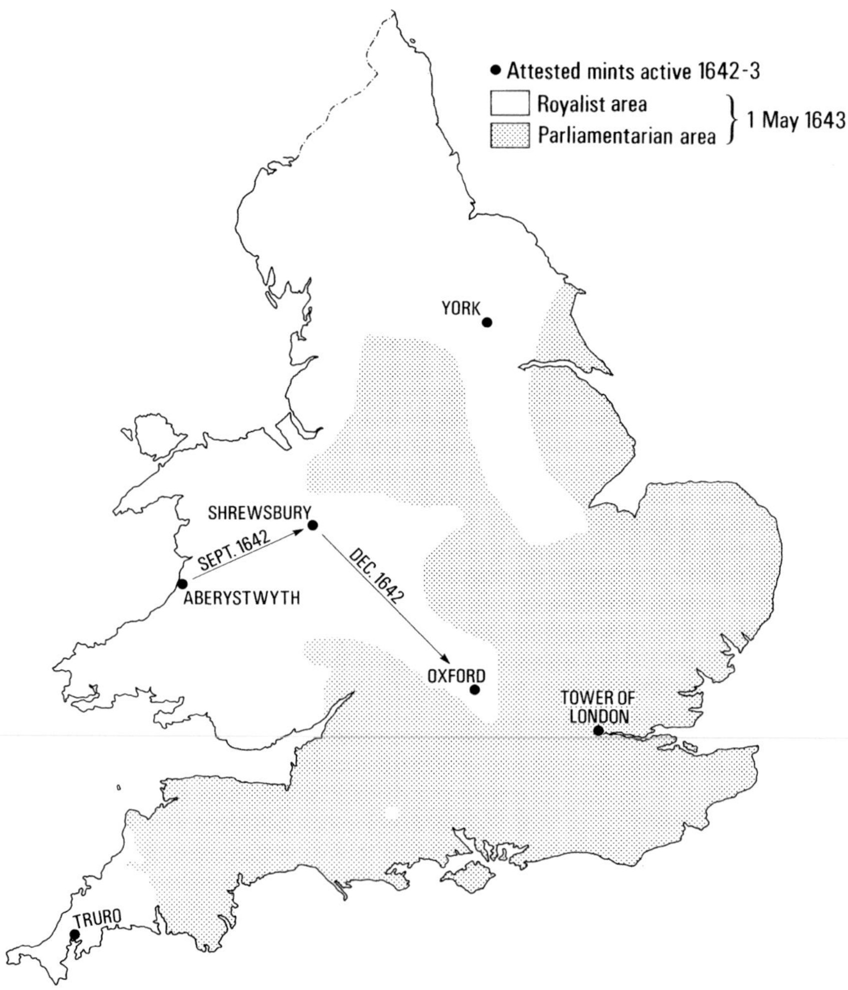

Map 2 The mints of the first campaigns, 1642-3.

Active steps were taken by the royalists to establish mints in the provinces from the moment the King and his court settled in York. Nicholas Briot was summoned to York and equipment was meanwhile prepared at the Tower Mint for use in proposed mints at Shrewsbury and York. These were to be campaign mints designed to help establish and equip the King's field army. In the event, York could as yet play no useful part, but Shrewsbury's contribution was valuable in both practical and propaganda terms. A third mint, at Truro, owed its existence to the isolation of royalist Cornwall in the early months of the war. It too had its moment of usefulness as a campaign mint in the spring of 1643. York, meanwhile, finally started production late in January 1643.

Although little documentation survives, enough remains to demonstrate the important point that the royalist mints were established with full formality. York mint was set up by royal warrant at the time that the court was based there; and the Earl of Newcastle's commission as Commander-in-Chief north of the Trent, issued in October 1642, included the power to coin money. Shrewsbury, and its successors at Oxford and then Bristol, operated as extensions of the Aberystwyth mint and no further authority was required. Thomas Bushell and Sir William Parkhurst, erstwhile Warden of the Tower Mint, were named joint wardens of this group of mints. In Cornwall, Sir Richard Vyvyan received a commission to coin bullion or plate in November 1642. The three areas of royalist power were thus formally equipped with the authority for coining.

After Edgehill, the Shrewsbury mint was moved to Oxford, arriving early in January 1643. Both sides had to make more permanent financial arrangements as the scale of the war grew. The money needed to finance each season's campaigns was raised in various ways: by local assessments in the counties; from traditional revenues such as the Court of Wards, where these could be enforced; from the Customs of ports such as Bristol; from the Excise, invented by the Parliament in 1643 and imitated by the royalists; and by appropriating the assets of 'delinquents', as each side described the other's supporters. There were other fund-raising attempts, notably in February 1644 when the King sent 'privy seal' letters to known supporters, in the hope of raising £100,000 for that year's campaign.

Developments in 1643 saw two major changes: a further branch mint of Aberystwyth was set up in Bristol from Oxford; and the Truro mint was transferred to Exeter, hard on the heels of the royalist capture of these cities. A new commission regularizing the Exeter mint was subsequently sent

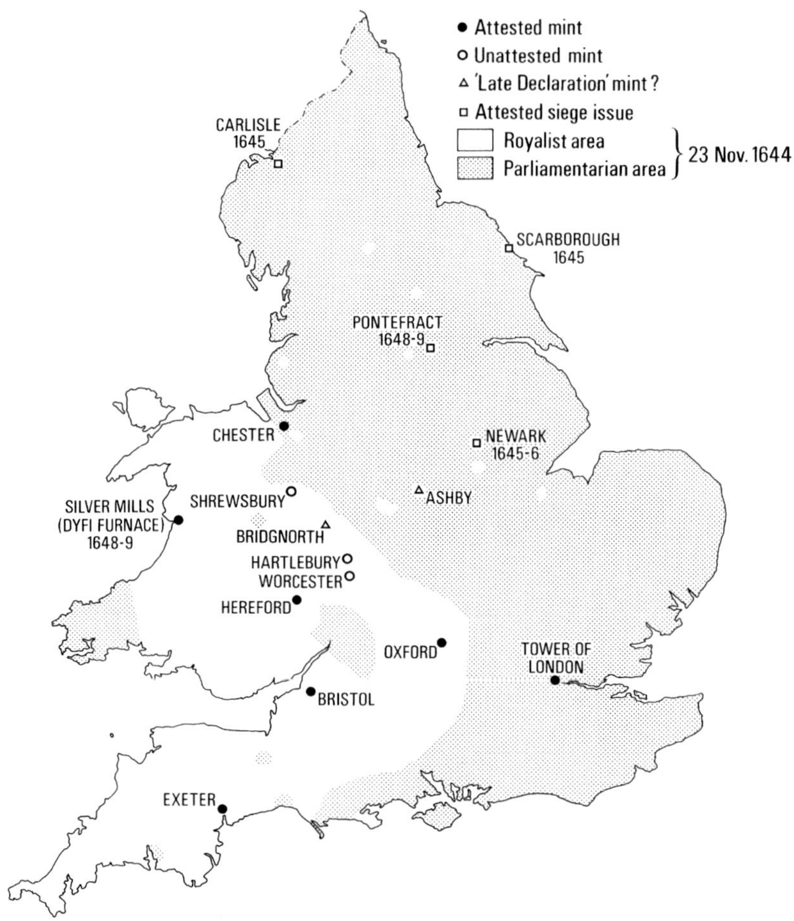

Map 3 Minting during the late stages of the war.

to Vyvyan (**4.2**). Next, on 22 May 1644, Sir Thomas Cary received a commission to erect one or more mints in the counties of Hereford, Worcester, Shropshire and Chester; it is likely, though unproved, that at least one mint operated in each (Hereford and Chester are attested by documents, Worcester and Salop (Shrewsbury) only by coins). This extension of royalist minting arrangements may have arisen from the administrative reforms carried out by Prince Rupert following his appointment as Captain-General in the Welsh Marches in January 1644, which included an overhaul of the operation of local taxation. A further commission dated 29 July 1644 was issued to Edward, Lord Herbert, to erect one or more mints (in South Wales, presumably) but was not acted upon. In 1660, in a letter to the Earl of Clarendon, Herbert (better known as the Earl of Glamorgan) explained that his commitment in Ireland (where he had been secretly empowered by the King to negotiate with the Irish Catholics) had prevented him from using his minting powers.

We do not know the wording of Newcastle's commission which set York into motion, but the terms of the others are generally similar. Vyvyan was required to use 'the like stamps and forme as the monies now current within our Realme of England' (November 1642) and more explicitly in his second commission (3 January 1644) 'to make and engrave … Irons and Stamps with Our Effigies Inscriptions and Armes according to our present money in Our Tower of London'. Cary was authorized to coin 'moneys in such manner as in the Tower of London'. In the event, both Vyvyan and Cary followed the extended provisions of Bushell's Aberystwyth indentures in producing groats and threepences in addition to normal Tower denominations; threepences were also produced at York. Only occasionally, and perhaps for special reasons, did they produce the *Exurgat* designs (see p.40) characteristic of the 'royal' series at Shrewsbury, Oxford and Bristol. For their pains, the royalist mint masters were granted the same allowances as were paid at the Tower, and without having to present their accounts. The local commander's note of receipt discharged the master's responsibilities.

Mint practice differed from that at the Tower in that there was no provision for a trial of the pyx, though Bushell's Aberystwyth indenture had included that check; nevertheless products were required to conform to Tower standards of weight and fineness, and from the middle of 1643, as the network grew, many royalist coins were marked with abbreviated mint names to distinguish their origins. Despite obvious temptation, efforts clearly were made to maintain the stipulated standards and significant debasement appears occasionally only late in the war, notably in the Cary series in the West. However, the fineness of articles of plate will have varied somewhat, making adhesion to the standards harder to achieve. Some silver was so poor that at Oxford Sir William Parkhurst was obliged to refine it before coining, while Thomas Bushell was able to use his highly-refined Welsh silver to improve the quality of mixed melts at Shrewsbury, Oxford (until mid-1643) and Bristol. Oxford's gold shows a progressive decline to around 20 carats fine. It is harder to be sure about the maintenance of weight standards because of the contemporary prevalence of clipping and the culling of overweight specimens. Discounting clipped coin, surviving royalist issues appear to be broadly comparable with Tower coins in range, but often falling short on average by a few per cent. At York, for instance, weights appear to fall on average about five per cent short of the standard, and vary considerably. This may relate to the experimental nature of the machinery used there, but could hint at a deliberate eking out of limited bullion, something seen more obviously in the emergency ('siege') coins issued by the defenders of Carlisle in 1645 (and some of those in the name of Charles II at Pontefract early in 1649).

The bulk of all business, on both sides, employed the Tower Mint money already in circulation, augmented by its continuing huge output. That of the royalist mints was by contrast feeble, but it usefully supplemented Tower coin in local transactions. Oxford's output went to the Treasurer at War, John Ashburnham; Vyvyan was required successively to deliver coin to Sir Ralph Hopton (1642), Hugh Hodges, Deputy Treasurer of the western army (November 1643) and Sir John Berkeley, Governor of Exeter (January 1644), while the products of Cary's mints went to Prince Rupert or his deputies. The 1985 Breckenbrough hoard included York coins in a deposit which may be related to the regular purchasing of provisions for the York garrison and Oxford issues accounted for one-fifth of a small hoard buried at Old Marston, just outside that city. Thus, the localized occurrence of royalist coins as attested by the wartime hoards can help to suggest the origins of those coins whose mints are not explicitly identified. For the most part, surviving coins may be attributed to the known mints. They are either marked, or fall into clear groups which can be related to securely-identified types. The larger mints produced a range of denominations including, occasionally, gold; it appears that there were also several smaller mints, output from which was restricted to half crowns (see Table III). Few of their sites can be identified and the rarity of their products hints at tiny output based on collected plate. They may have operated at local tax-collecting centres as branches of the authorized mints, each equipped with a simple coining machine, operation of which required no great skill, as is evident from their products.

The late stages of the war saw a succession of sieges as isolated royalist garrisons were reduced. In some there was little need for money, but at Carlisle, Scarborough and Newark emergency money was issued by authority of the Governor. These coinages were purely local and of distinctive designs, as was that of the defenders of Pontefract during its extended siege in 1648-9. Meanwhile the mint-cities themselves were isolated and taken, beginning with York in July 1644. Their tiny output, compared with the uninterrupted flood from the Tower, has been mentioned. The royalist mints – even Oxford, the biggest – were of so small account that none is mentioned in any articles of surrender. However, minting tools were seized. On 14 July 1646, three weeks after Oxford's surrender, Sir Robert Harley and others were ordered by the Commons to search 'Trunks lately come from Oxon' for 'instruments, and other materials and things belonging to the mint, or fit to be made use of in the coinage of money', to be seized and reported to the House for disposal. Lists survive of tools and dies surrendered at Exeter in 1646 and at the Silver Mills (Dyfi Furnace), the post-war revival of Aberystwyth, in 1649.

Table III: *The pattern of royalist minting, 1642-6*

	GOLD			SILVER									
	£3	20s	10s	20s	10s	5s	2s 6d	1s	6d	4d	3d	2d	1d
Bushell/Parkhurst													
Shrewsbury, 1642	?			*	*	*	*	*					
Oxford, 1642-3	*	*	*	*	*	*	*	*	*		?	?	?
Oxford, 1644-6	*	*	*	*		*	*	*	*	*	*	*	*
Bristol, 1643-5		*	*				*	*	*	*	*	*	*
A/B/plumes, 1645-6							*	*	*	*	*	*	?
Vyvyan													
Truro, 1642-3		?	*			*	*	*					
Exeter, 1643-6		*			*	*	*	*	*	*	*	*	*
Newcastle/Martin													
York, 1643-4							*	*	*		*		
Cary													
W/SA series, 1644-6		*					*	*	*	*	*	*	
Chester, 1644-5		*					*	*			*		
HC							*						
CH							*						
'Declaration'							*						
'Garter', 1645							*						

Chapter 3

THE KING'S MINT

The value of a provincial mint with a loyal master may have been foreseen by Charles I when he authorized its establishment. Aberystwyth's last delivery of coined money was entered in Bushell's account book on 20 September 1642. The furnaces were drawn and the mint was on the move, summoned to Shrewsbury by the King to coin the plate he hoped his supporters would provide. The following year was to see two more transfers for Bushell: to Oxford, which became the King's main mint, and then to Bristol where until September 1645 he ran the branch mint set up after the royalist capture of that city. The distinctive products of the 'royal' mints of the Civil War will be described in the order in which the mints were established.

Shrewsbury mint

In this same town of Sirosberi his Majesty has set them to work these last days in melting down old silver plate ... He has had all this coined into money to supply the pay of the army and other expenses required.

Upon receipt of the King's summons, Thomas Bushell closed the Aberystwyth mint and moved its equipment and staff to Shrewsbury, probably arriving around the end of the month – on the 28th the King, speaking of having 'sent hither for a mint', still awaited it. Bushell may have been joined there by Sir William Parkhurst, Warden of the Tower Mint. Work presumably started at the beginning of October, perhaps in the castle (**3.1**), though our earliest reference comes in a letter from the Venetian ambassador in London, Giovanni Giustinian, quoted above, written on 14 October. Four days later, a local inhabitant wrote in a letter: 'the mint is come to our town, and one Master Bushell doth coin every day, for abundance of plate is sent in to the King from the several counties about us...'

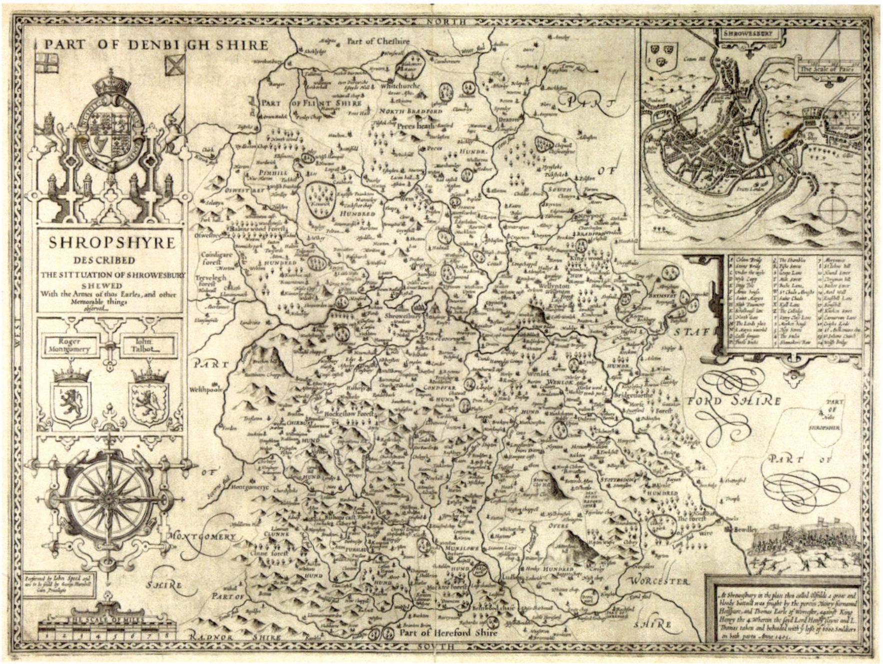

Fig. 3.1 John Speed's Map of Shropshire (1616), with a vignette of Shrewsbury showing the town's position in a loop of the river Severn, guarded to landward by the castle. *Llyfrgell Genedlaethol Cymru/National Library of Wales*.

The mint had brought some of its dies with it and its first products may have been of purely Aberystwyth type – one late 'Aberystwyth' shilling in the National Museum of Wales appears from its metal to have been made from plate; other coins 'mule' Aberystwyth and Shrewsbury designs (**3.4**). Facing for the first time the necessity of producing its own dies, the mint's enthusiastic improvisation gave us the most characteristic royalist coinage of the war, known to contemporaries as 'Exurgat money' (**3.2**, **3.3**, **3.5**). On the reverse, in place of the royal arms, the King's aims as declared at Wellington on 19 September were set out in their abbreviated Latin form: RELIG:PROT:LEG:ANGL:LIBER:PAR ('The Protestant Religion, the Laws of England, the Liberty of Parliament'), surrounded by verse 1 of Psalm 68: EXVRGAT DEVS DISSIPENTVR INIMICI ('Let God arise, let his enemies be scattered'), a Vulgate tag familiar from the early coins of James I. Welsh feathers, the date (unusual on contemporary English coin-

Fig. 3.2 Silver twenty shillings, Shrewsbury 1642. The largest silver type ever struck in England, this 'medal' weighs about 120 grammes, or nearly four Troy ounces. The equestrian portrait is made from the same punch as that of the silver crown, 1.25, purloined from the Tower. The reverse die was used again at Oxford (see 3.8).

Fig. 3.3 Half crown, Shrewsbury 1642, showing the locally-engraved 'Shrewsbury horseman'. *Tregwynt Treasure Trove*

Fig. 3.4 Half crown, Shrewsbury, undated (1642); struck using a reverse die brought from Aberystwyth.

Fig. 3.5 Shilling, Shrewsbury 1642. Small numbers of shillings were struck at Shrewsbury, mostly using an Aberystwyth obverse die, as here; another shilling die, bearing a very crude portrait, was engraved locally.

age) and on some dies the value fill out a distinctive design. A local man, Edward Bott, may have played a part in their production.

As early as 21 October, the design was known in London, as reported in a further letter from Giustinian to the Doge and Senate:

> Upon the money coined at Sirosberi the King has had another motto printed instead of the usual inscription, to wit Exurgat Deus et Dissipentur inimici ejus, and another in the middle Pro Religione et Parliamento [*sic*], all in order to make it more and more patent to his people that his intentions are directed solely to the preservation of religion and the privileges of the country and remote from those ambitious designs which for their own purposes are put abroad by those who have been the authors of the plan to bring a prince of such blameless habits to a state so deplorable.

The message of the new royal coins was clearly understood.

The same day, at Wolverhampton, Bushell distributed around £2,000 worth of the new money to the royal army '… to each Colonell, the medall of a 20s piece of silver, all the other Officers ten or five, and each Private Soldier Half a Crown', as an advance of pay before Edgehill. These 'medalls' may be identified with the massive silver denominations of the Exurgat money (**3.2**). They may have been produced because of a shortage of gold for the normal ten- and twenty-shilling pieces, but the name 'medall' also no doubt circumvented Bushell's lack of authority to strike *coins* larger than a half crown. Nevertheless, these large silver pieces adhered strictly to contemporary weight standards, the twenty-shillings each weighing nearly four Troy ounces.

After the inconclusive battle at Edgehill on 23 October (both sides claimed a victory, though the Parliament retired from the field) the mint remained at Shrewsbury until December, when it was ordered to Oxford, which in the meantime had become the King's wartime headquarters.

Oxford mint

We hear that assistance in men and plate is constantly reaching the King …He proposes to establish another [mint] at Oxford for coining this silver.

Gerolamo Agostini, Venetian Secretary, writing on 20 January 1643, was for once behind the times. On 20 December, Bushell had passed through Bridgnorth, where the bailiffs bestowed 'a quarter of sack and a quarter of burnt claret' upon him; on Tuesday 3 January, a young Anthony Wood had noted,

> There came into Oxford and to the court, diverse carts, to the number of 12 or more, loaden with Prince Rupert's gooddes, and with the mint from Shrewsbury, and with some good store of silver ore, to be melted into silver and coyned into money: one Mr Bushell being the cheife dealer therein; the mint was set up in the New Inne.

New Inn Hall (today St Peter's College, **3.6**), a 'nest of puritans' abandoned by its inhabitants, had been requisitioned for the purpose in mid-December. The King lost little time: on 6 January a circular letter to all colleges sought raw material for the mint:

> We are soe well satisfied with your readyness and affection to our service that wee cannot doubt but that you will take all occasions to

> express the same, etc … and having received severall quantityes of plate from divers of our loving subjects, we have removed our Mint hither to our Citty of Oxford for the coyning thereof. And we do hereby desire you, that you will send unto Us all such Plate of what kind soever, which belongs to your College, promising you to see the same justly repayed to you after the rate of 5s the ounce for white and 5s 6d for gilt Plate, as soone as God shall enable us…

Fig. 3.6 New Inn Hall, Oxford, from David Loggan, *Oxonia Illustrata …*, 1675. © *Society of Antiquaries of London*

Collection was entrusted to 'our trusty and welbeloved Sr William Parkhurst Knt and Thomas Bushell Esq. Officers of our Mint'. Twelve colleges complied, with contributions ranging from 41 lb (Balliol) to 296 lb (Magdalen). St John's, hoping to save its plate, sent its value in money, but the King was not deflected: he sent a second time to demand the plate and had it, 224 lb 4 oz in all.

The only real resistance came from Exeter, the West Country college, which replied that to hand over its plate, upon any pretext, would be contrary to its statutes. On 28 January the King replied through the Master of Requests, Sir Thomas Aylesbury, reiterating his claims on the college's loyalty: in effect they were all in the same boat. Exeter's rearguard action continued with the following submission:

> The Rector and ffellowes of Exeter College uppon serious consideration of His Majestie's gratious answere to their humble petition are ready to satisfy his desire & obey his commandes concerning their plate expressed in his Royal letters of the 6th of Jan 1642[*3*]. But with these humble desires, which they trust his Majesty will bee pleased gratiously to assent to.

1. That in regard of the great quantity of plate which they are to part withall and the poverty of the colledge, a debt of 138 l. which they have incurred by means of their late loan to his Majesty may be satisfied out of the money arising from their plate, and that his Majesty would be pleased to grant a warrant that it may be taken up out of the Mint now in Oxford
2. That a reservation be made of their communion plate, which they are persuaded his Majesty intends not to make use of.
3. That some time bee allowed them for taking out the names and titles of the severall donors, together with the weight of the severall pieces, that so their memories, as they well deserved, may be preserved to posterity.

On the 30th the King conceded the last two requests – communion plate was generally spared – but would not budge on the debt:

> But his Majesty hopes, shortly to be able to make a full repayment both for this plate, and the money formerly lent to Him, that soe the College may not only pay the debt of £138 owing by them, but have their Treasury repaired, besides the conscience of having so seasonably served and supplied his Majesty.

And that was the end of it. Three days later 246 lb of plate, the third largest college consignment, duly recorded in *A Register of severall pieces of Plate lent to the King ffeb: 2 1642 towards the supply of his Majestie's extraordinary necessity at that time*, was handed over.

Four of Charles I's mint masters were involved, however indirectly, in the story of Exeter College's plate. Bushell and Parkhurst signed for it (**3.7**), melted it and coined it. Sir Thomas Aylesbury, Master of Requests and joint master of the Tower Mint, had been ejected by Parliament in 1642; he followed the King to Oxford, where he continued to hold the Court of Requests. He was to die in comparative poverty in Breda in 1657, aged 81. And the fourth? Among the many entries in the *Register*, which survives, we may note a tankard of white plate, weighing 28 oz 1 dwt, which bore the following inscription:

> *Ex dono Ricardi Vyvian – ffrancisci Vyvian Equitis*
> *Aurati filii natu maximi, et hujus Collegii Commensalis 1628*

enough silver to pay a cavalryman for nearly two months could the future Truro and Exeter mint master have but known.

Apart from chapel plate, little was excepted. An ostrich egg mounted in silver-gilt belonging to Exeter College was spared, for instance, presumably on account of its small value, while one notable survivor is the 42-ounce 'Founder's Cup' belonging to Magdalen College. This silver-gilt covered cup, made *c*. 1601-3, but surmounted by a figure of St Mary Magdalene which had perhaps come from a vessel of the time of its founder, William Waynflete (d. 1486), was saved at the last moment when Dr Accepted Frewen, the College's President, bought it back from Sir William Parkhurst for its full value, £11 11s 6d. Frewen probably removed it from Oxford in 1644 when appointed Bishop of Lichfield and was able to return it to the College after the Restoration.

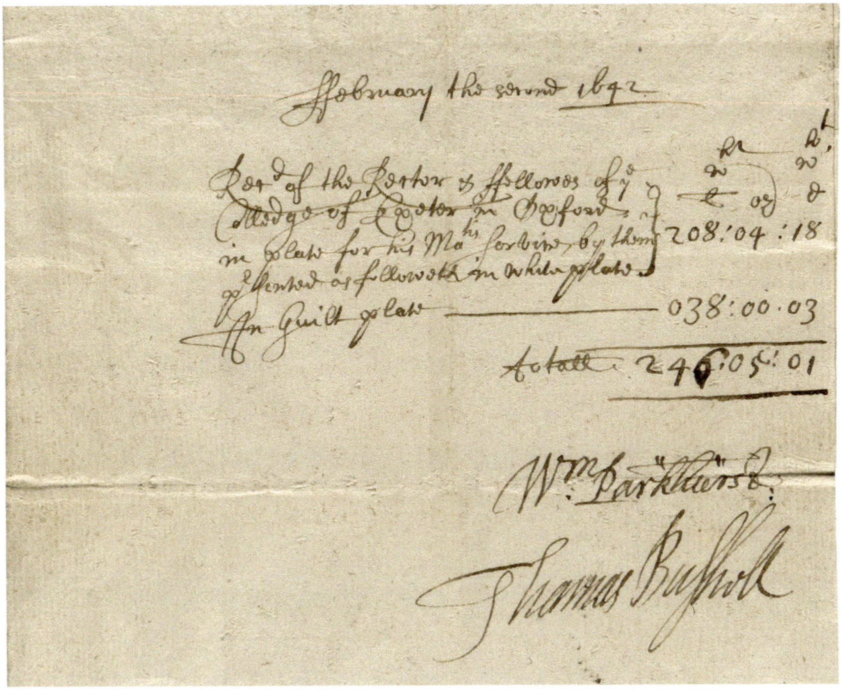

Fig. 3.7 Oxford plate: receipt signed by Parkhurst and Bushell, 2 February 1643 (dated OS 1642), for 246 lb of gilt and white plate surrendered reluctantly by Exeter College 'for his Majesty's service'. *Exeter College Archives, Charles I correspondence; published with permission of the Rector and Scholars of Exeter College, Oxford*

So, by early February 1643, plate to the value of about £8,500 (2,782 lb 9 oz 8 dwt, including contributions from the gentry and clergy), plus unknown amounts from the four other colleges and the Oxford Halls, had reached the mint. This and the £100 or so per week of Welsh silver received until the late summer presumably formed the bulk of the £13,188 14s 6d received 'from your Majesty's Mynt at divers payments' by the Treasurer at War, John Ashburnham, between November 1642 and October 1643. Total output was probably higher, for Ashburnham accounts separately for £640-worth of silver plate, such as three dozen trenchers worth £89 from Lady Horwood and a gold chain valued at £105 (about two and a half pounds Troy) looted from a prominent parliamentarian, Sir John Wilde.

Other contributions included plate, since Ashburnham occasionally had to make up the losses in coining its variable quality, but we have no means of quantifying these. It seems certain, though, that estimates suggesting that Oxford's output was measured in hundreds of thousands of pounds are, to put it mildly, exaggerations.

In the late summer of 1643, Thomas Bushell was sent to Bristol to establish a branch mint, leaving Parkhurst in charge at Oxford. Other members of the Oxford staff may be identified: Robert Hunt, who died in Oxford in October 1643, had been with Bushell at Aberystwyth, presumably seconded from the Tower, and may therefore also have worked at Shrewsbury. Edward Maynard, a former Tower moneyer, returned to London in 1644 and petitioned the Committee for Compounding, admitting having worked at Oxford; fined £50, he is recorded again at the Tower in 1653. Richard Nicholls served Bushell as head moneyer at Shrewsbury, Oxford and Bristol; also, at the Tower under the Commonwealth. Oxford also saw the emergence of the talents of Thomas Rawlins, playwright and sometime pupil of Nicholas Briot, who was appointed Graver of Seals, Stamps and Medals in 1643 and (nominally) chief graver in the Tower of London and elsewhere in England and Wales in April 1645, no doubt in response to Parliament's promotion of Thomas Simon and Edward Wade. Rawlins' most famous work is the 1644 crown (**3.20**) but he was also responsible *inter alia* for the obverse of the fine silver twenty shillings dated 1642 (**3.8**), a portrait medal of Parkhurst (**3.18**) and the elegant gold £3 pieces of 1643-44 (**3.21**).

Because the New Year was reckoned from Lady Day (25 March) the early Oxford products, like those of Shrewsbury, bore the date 1642. Telling the two apart can be difficult, but is conventionally achieved by noting the form of the 'Welsh' feathers badge which on virtually all Oxford coins marked 'OX' and dated 1643 or later (e.g., **3.19**) bears labels or 'bands' for the Prince of Wales's motto (the motto itself is not expressed because of the small scale). Those coins dated 1642 with this form of the badge are therefore regarded as Oxford products and the others without bands are ascribed to Shrewsbury. That this distinction is broadly correct would appear to be

Fig. 3.8 Silver twenty shillings, Oxford, dated 1642 [OS]. The equestrian portrait by Rawlins is one of the finest pieces of English die-engraving of the period. See 3.2 for the earlier use of the reverse die at Shrewsbury.

confirmed by the adoption of a third form of the badge on coins made at Bristol (see the section headings in this chapter). Some of Shrewsbury's dies, however, continued in use at Oxford, if indeed they were not made at Oxford to the same pattern to start with, as a gold £3 piece may suggest.

Oxford was the only royalist mint to coin significant quantities of gold, the raw material coming from jewellery and personal ornaments such as Sir John Wilde's chain. Twenty- and ten-shillings pieces matched contemporary Tower standards, but the propaganda value of royal gifts was not neglected. In February 1643 a magnificent £3 piece was introduced (**3.9**) and the message of the King's 'new coin' spread by a specially-printed pamphlet which included ink impressions of its dies. One pair of dies dated 1642 bears 'Shrewsbury' feathers, all others the Oxford form. In silver there was a full range of denominations from the penny up to the great twenty-shilling pieces (**3.8**). The characteristic coin, here as elsewhere, was the half crown (**3.19**, **3.23**). All but the smallest coins are normally of 'Exurgat'

Fig. 3.9 Gold £3 piece, Oxford, dated 1642. By far the largest English denomination of the time, perhaps used for royal gifts. The King's sword and olive branch offer a symbolic choice between war and peace.

Fig. 3.10 Silver crown, Oxford 1643, with a new equestrian effigy usually described today as the 'Oxford horseman'.

Fig. 3.11 Shilling, Oxford 1643.

Fig. 3.12 Sixpence, Oxford 1643, using an Aberystwyth obverse die.

type and some of the smaller denominations, which had not been produced at Shrewsbury, were made using dies brought from Aberystwyth (**3.12**).

Another feature of the mint's activity during 1643 was the production of medals, the only royalist mint to do so. There was plenty to celebrate: the reunion of the King and his Queen on 13 July after eighteen months' separation and the capture of Bristol, the kingdom's second largest port, on 26 July form the subjects of medals which are very rare today (**3.13**). Rarer still are three military and civil awards attested by royal warrants: firstly, a projected medal in gold to reward 'our true hearted subjects from our county of Salop' in January 1643; secondly, on 18 May, a silver badge for the 'forlorn hope'; and thirdly on 1 June, gold medals to reward personal valour at Edgehill (somewhat belated, though knighthoods had been awarded on the spot) to Captain John Smith and to Robert Welch. (Smith had recovered the royal standard, Welch those of the King's Lifeguard of Foot, lost in the heat of the battle.) Smith and Welch are reported to have worn their medals 'on a green watered ribbon across the shoulders'. Neither survives, nor is a specimen of the Shropshire medal known, but the appearance of Welch's medal is known from a drawing made in 1685 (**3.14**). An intact specimen of the Forlorn Hope badge has, however, been identified (**3.15**). All three awards, if all were indeed made, seem to have employed the same die, an early Rawlins effort depicting Charles I and Prince Charles. Welch's medal appears to have had an engraved reverse.

The Forlorn Hope badge was awarded to members of advance parties in engagements, who might be horse, dragoons or foot. It was a simple shell, with no reverse, designed for wear on the breast, sewn to clothing or a sash. The badge may have been introduced as a morale-booster for the rank and file – the idea seems to have come from Bushell; there were soon plenty of engagements, notably in the West, which might justify its award, though how many were made cannot be known. The warrant (**3.16**) was printed and distributed to commanders and foreshadows remarkably the practices of more recent years: a need is identified, an award created, its design specified and conditions laid down regarding recommendation, the

Fig.3.13 Oxford medals, 1643, by Rawlins: the first commemorates the reunion of King Charles I and Queen Henrietta Maria (returned from the Continent via York and Newark – see p.103) on the field of Edgehill, near Kineton, Warwickshire, 13 July 1643. The meeting and the 'defeat of the rebels in the West' (at Roundway Down, Wiltshire) on the same day are seen as an omen of victory and peace. The second celebrates the capture of Bristol, 26 July; compare with 3.24. *Courtesy of the Trustees of the British Museum*

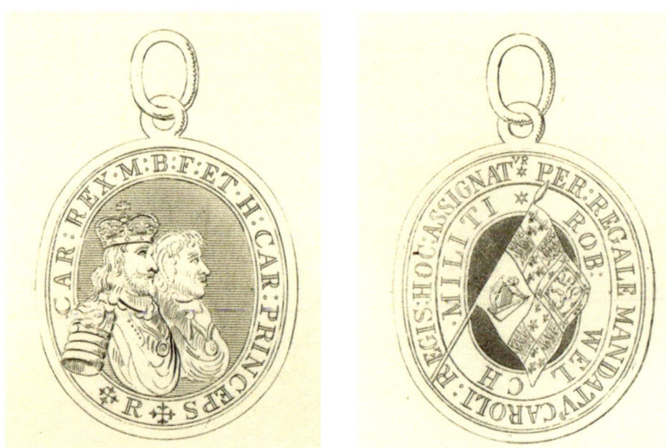

Fig. 3.14 The gold medal awarded to Sir Robert Welch for his services at Edgehill, 23 October 1642, as recorded in a document of 1685. From Numismatic Chronicle xv (1853). *By permission of the Royal Numismatic Society.*

Fig. 3.15 Silver badge for the Forlorn Hope, 1643. This corresponds in almost every detail to the woodcut on the warrant (3.16), with the addition of TR in monogram, for Thomas Rawlins. It has no reverse, since it was designed for wear on the breast, sewn to a sash or the recipient's tunic (hence the holes in the rim).

keeping of registers (though none survives) and safeguards against abuse. In several ways, this badge occupies an important, if neglected place in the history of British awards and honours.

Rawlins was also responsible for a considerable number of non-specific royalist medals or badges, such as **3.17**. As fortunes declined, there was less to celebrate and no more medals, apart from Rawlins' splendid 1644 portrait of Sir William Parkhurst (**3.18**). The early months of 1644 may have been busy at the Oxford mint, since in February the King appealed by letter to selected supporters to contribute towards £100,000 needed for that year's campaign. How much was raised is not known, but surviving receipts suggest that a proportion was paid in plate. This was also the year of Rawlins' masterpiece, the 'Oxford crown' (**3.20**).

The ceremony of 'touching for the King's evil' seems to have been maintained during the war. Hitherto, specially-made angels in fine gold were hung round the necks of the sufferers, suspended from a white ribbon. The last angels were made in London in 1641-2, so other arrangements became necessary. An Oxford gold ten-shillings of 1643, found near Priston (N. Somerset) in November 2013, has a large hole that might indicate its

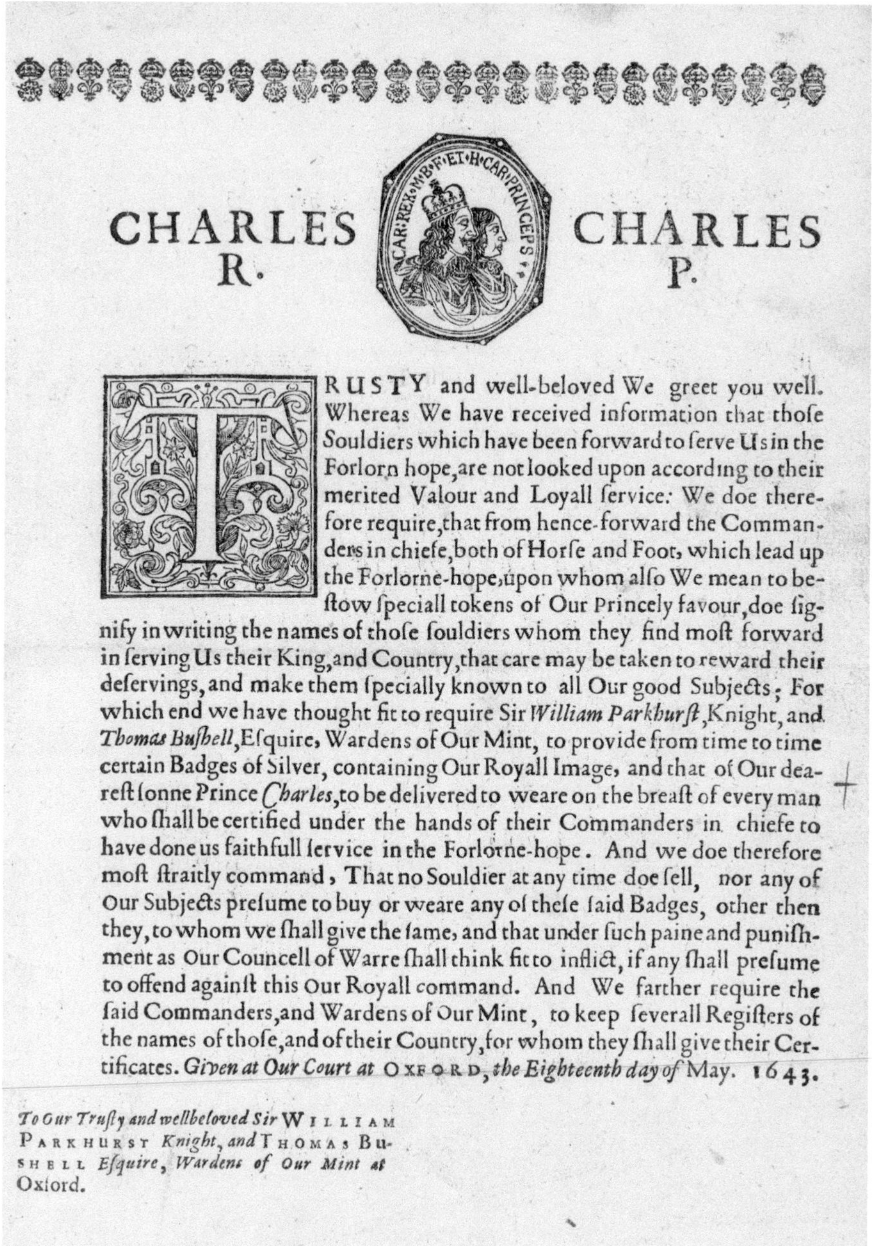

CHARLES R. CHARLES P.

TRUSTY and well-beloved We greet you well. Whereas We have received information that thoſe Souldiers which have been forward to ſerve Us in the Forlorn hope, are not looked upon according to their merited Valour and Loyall ſervice: We doe therefore require, that from hence-forward the Commanders in chiefe, both of Horſe and Foot, which lead up the Forlorne-hope, upon whom alſo We mean to beſtow ſpeciall tokens of Our Princely favour, doe ſignify in writing the names of thoſe ſouldiers whom they find moſt forward in ſerving Us their King, and Country, that care may be taken to reward their deſervings, and make them ſpecially known to all Our good Subjects; For which end we have thought fit to require Sir *William Parkhurſt*, Knight, and *Thomas Buſhell*, Eſquire, Wardens of Our Mint, to provide from time to time certain Badges of Silver, containing Our Royall Image, and that of Our deareſt ſonne Prince *Charles*, to be delivered to weare on the breaſt of every man who ſhall be certified under the hands of their Commanders in chiefe to have done us faithfull ſervice in the Forlorne-hope. And we doe therefore moſt ſtraitly command, That no Souldier at any time doe ſell, nor any of Our Subjects preſume to buy or weare any of theſe ſaid Badges, other then they, to whom we ſhall give the ſame, and that under ſuch paine and puniſhment as Our Councell of Warre ſhall think fit to inflict, if any ſhall preſume to offend againſt this Our Royall command. And We farther require the ſaid Commanders, and Wardens of Our Mint, to keep ſeverall Regiſters of the names of thoſe, and of their Country, for whom they ſhall give their Certificates. *Given at Our Court at* OXFORD, *the Eighteenth day of* May. 1643.

To Our Truſty and wellbeloved Sir WILLIAM PARKHURST *Knight, and* THOMAS BUSHELL *Eſquire, Wardens of Our Mint at* Oxford.

Fig. 3.16 Arch. Ash. Fol. MS. 56 Printed warrant for silver badges for the Forlorn Hope, Oxford 18 May 1643. *Image © Ashmolean Museum, University of Oxford.*

Fig. 3.17 Cast silver badge with loop for suspension, by Rawlins, *c*.1643-5.

Fig. 3.18 Sir William Parkhurst, by Rawlins, Oxford 1644. The Oxford mint master is holding a badge similar to 3.17. The National Museum of Wales's specimen consists of a silver 'shell' mounted in the centre of an eighteenth-century pewter dish. Actual diameter = 80 mm. Parkhurst's character is clearly seen: a 'very honest gentleman', according to Lady Fanshawe in 1645, while the same year the dispossessed Yorkshire royalist Sir Henry Slingsby 'had my quarters with Sir Wm Parkhurst the mint master. I lived here with great ease and much content, through Sir Wm Parkhurst his noble entertainment.' All this in the crowded and chaotic conditions of wartime Oxford!

Fig. 3.19 Half crown, Oxford 1644, with signature OX. The posture of the horseman on the later Oxford silver resembles that on Briot's experimental issues (e.g. 1.22). *Penybryn Treasure Trove*

Fig. 3.20 Crown, 1644 OX, by Rawlins. A more accomplished, if less lively horseman than 3.8, framing a view of Oxford after the manner of contemporary Continental coins, depicting churches, colleges and the city's fortifications. Signed 'R' (obverse, lower left). It is sometimes held to be a pattern, but the number surviving and the poor production standard of some of them suggest that a substantive issue was intended. *Spink & Son Ltd.*

Fig. 3.21 Gold £3 piece, Oxford 1644, the last year in which these coins were struck. *Courtesy of the Trustees of the British Museum*

use for the ceremony (**3.22**). In February 1647, as the king was brought south having been handed over to Parliament by the Scots, people came to be touched, bringing their own coins – of gold or of silver – and ribbons; a holed Tower Mint gold ten shillings, privy-mark Sun, in the Brooker collection (pl.XVII, 174) might represent such a coin.

Oxford's coins appear to have been made by manual striking methods – evidence of multiple blows rules out rotary techniques, but it is quite possible that some form of mechanical assistance, such as a drop hammer, could have been used to help make the larger denominations. Analyses have demonstrated that in general Oxford silver coins are of good silver and full weight – its staff were the most experienced of all Charles's wartime mints. The gold does seem to show a gentle but progressive debasement from 22 down to around 20 carats. Both metals show a decline in 1644-5, which was also a period of relatively low output; this may reflect the state of royalist finances, or Parkhurst's attested difficulties, perhaps compounded by a serious fire in October 1644 in the mint's part of Oxford, supposedly caused by a soldier roasting a stolen pig. Coins dated 1646 (i.e. those produced between 25 March and 24 June 1646, when the city surrendered) are surprisingly common (**3.23**), however, perhaps because the siege of Oxford restricted their circulation and encouraged their retention as souvenirs.

Fig. 3.22 Ten shillings, Oxford 1643. A cherished souvenir: both bent as a 'love token' and with a sizeable hole which may indicate its use in a wartime ceremony of 'touching' for scrofula at Oxford. *By courtesy of the Portable Antiquities Scheme, WILT-852CB5.*

Fig. 3.23 Half crown, Oxford 1646. Note that the King's effigy has been deliberately defaced, an act of spite occasionally paralleled on coins of other rulers, notably those of Louis XVI of France, decapitated in 1793.

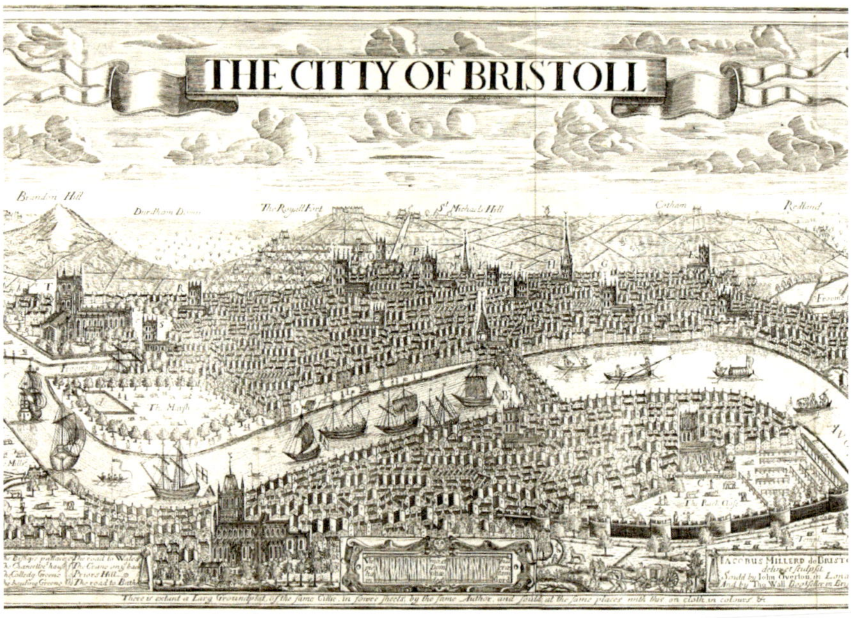

Fig. 3.24 Bristol, from the south: the central portion of James Millerd's panoramic view, 1673. The castle had been demolished in 1656, but Bristol Bridge, with its houses, may be seen in the centre. In the foreground are the southern defences, which repulsed both royalist and parliamentarian troops, in 1643 and 1645 respectively. 'The Royall Fort' marks the site of the largest of a chain of outworks which protected the city's northern approaches. *Courtesy of Bristol Museum & Art Gallery.*

Bristol mint

The capture of Bristol, then England's second-largest city, on 26 July 1643 gave the royalists a much-needed major port and its potential economic importance to them helps to explain the establishment there of a branch mint derived from Oxford, probably by the autumn. Thomas Bushell was sent to Bristol and later claimed to have spent £1,020 repairing the castle and setting up the mint within it. Bushell himself took lodgings on Bristol Bridge, then lined with tall houses (**3.24**), with an apothecary, Mr Edwards, perhaps a relation of the Bristol merchant John Edwards, who was one of Bushell's partners in the Welsh mines. His regular shipments of Welsh silver were until late in 1644 diverted to Bristol *via* Swansea (it was the loss of these that forced Parkhurst at Oxford to refine silver to uphold the standard) and there may well have been prize goods in the spring of 1645 as well as continuing contributions in plate. After Bristol fell again in September 1645, Bushell

Fig. 3.25 Half crown, Bristol 1643. A typical early Bristol coin, with horseman similar to Oxford (e.g. 3.10) and BR monogram on the reverse.

Fig. 3.26 Half crown, Bristol 1644, signed BR in monogram on both sides; An unusually well struck example.

Fig. 3.27 Bristol, smaller denominations: sixpence 1644; threepence 1644; half groat, undated. The threepence is struck from an Aberystwyth obverse die.

Fig. 3.28 Gold twenty shillings, Bristol 1645. A handsome and carefully made coin for Court use.

Fig. 3.29 Shilling, Bristol 1645: compare with 3.30 and 3.32.

left a trunk of 'writings' there and the loss of these in a fire on 17 February 1647 presumably accounts for the complete lack of documentation relating to the functioning of the wartime mint; we are left with Bristol's products. Some early Bristol coins are similar to Oxford's (several Oxford dies were taken to Bristol) but they may be distinguished by the form of the 'Declaration', which is more condensed (RELIG:PROT:LE:AN:LI:PA:) and the *Exurgat* legend, which here begins at the top of the design (**3.25**).

The Bristol 'feathers', too, are distinctive, with the label intertwined with the stems of the ostrich plumes. Bushell's engraver soon evolved a characteristic style and the dies were marked BR in monogram (**3.26**). Rudimentary blank preparation and unskilled striking gave half crowns of a somewhat rough-and-ready appearance, sometimes squarish in shape. The smaller denominations were carefully made; a former Aberystwyth die was used to strike threepences in 1644 (**3.27**). Pride of place in the Bristol series belongs to the gold twenty-shilling pieces of 1645, which were probably struck for court use during Prince Charles's stay at Bristol as nominal head of the royalists in the West (**3.28**). At the other extreme, it was reported in the House of Commons in September 1644 that the royalists were making farthing tokens at Bristol, allegedly for troops' pay. Any such issues cannot be distinguished today; the large-scale use of tokens for pay is inherently unlikely, since their currency was strictly limited, to a maximum of sixpence-worth in a transaction of ten shillings, or one penny in a shilling.

'Late Declaration' coinage

Bristol surrendered to Fairfax on 11 September 1645, by which time Bushell had probably already retired to Lundy Isle, off the north Devon coast, which he was to hold until the end of the war. His moneyers, however, appear to have continued to work until the final months, using altered Bristol dies and others of similar type, perhaps at three locations, for their products are distinguished by the letters A (until recently only known on coins dated 1645) or B or by a small plume of feathers (both 1646; **3.31**, **3.32**).

In keeping with royalist practice, these letters and the feathers symbol are likely to denote different mints and there have been various attempts to identify these. Of possible Welsh mints, Aberystwyth (where a small coining of silver, otherwise unidentified, took place in January 1646 [if dated these would have read '1645']) and Beaumaris have been suggested;

Fig. 3.30 Shilling, 1645 A. Found at Clywedog, near Dolgellau, Merioneth *c*.1940.

Fig. 3.31 Sixpence, 1646 B.

Fig. 3.32 Shilling and threepence, 1646 'feathers'. The shilling obverse is an altered Bristol die, on which the BR monogram before 'CAROLVS' may still be discerned beneath the feathers mark.

Fig. 3.33 Half crown, 1646 A: a unique pairing of an 'A' die with a reverse die dated 1646. *Tregwynt Treasure Trove*

in the west Appledore and Barnstaple, both in north Devon. By the autumn of 1645 these areas, together with parts of the Midlands and the Welsh Marches, were all that remained in royalist hands. Six find spots are known for these 'Late Declaration' coins: a single find near Dolgellau (Gwynedd: **3.30**), and in hoards from Telford (Shropshire), High Ackworth (Wakefield), Middleham (N. Yorkshire) and Tregwynt (Pembrokeshire) for 'A' coins and a hoard from an imprecise location near Pershore, Worcestershire for a shilling of the 'feathers' group. These suggest that a West Country source is unlikely.

In 1981, George C. Boon made out a coherent case, based on known royalist troop movements, for identifying the first two mints as Ashby-de-la-Zouch, Leicestershire and Bridgnorth, Shropshire, both important garrisons which survived until late in the war. Minting equipment could well have been conveyed from Bristol to Oxford and thence to Ashby, which received reinforcements from Oxford late in September 1645. In turn, when Ashby surrendered on honourable terms on 28 February 1646, its garrison had liberty to march away to Bridgnorth or Worcester. Bridgnorth was held until 26 April, which would have given enough time for an issue of coins marked 1646 B. The discovery in the Tregwynt hoard (in 1996) of a half crown combining the 'A' obverse with a reverse dated 1646 (**3.33**) has re-opened this question, since all of Ashby's issues (if it was indeed the 'A' mint) would be expected to be dated 1645, Old Style. The reverse of the Tregwynt coin bears no privy-mark – signifying a mint of no fixed location? What does appear to be the case, though, is that all coins of this series that have been analysed appear to be made from silver of high fineness, above sterling (i.e., >92.5% fine), a characteristic of Bushell's freshly-refined Welsh silver.

Chapter 4

SIR RICHARD VYVYAN'S MINTS

When war broke out in August 1642, the royalists attempted to secure the West Country; they failed utterly. The Marquess of Hertford and Sir Ralph Hopton were chased out of Somerset and North Dorset, Hertford escaping across the Bristol Channel to Cardiff; Hopton, with a small body of dragoons and horse, retired to Cornwall. There, accused of disturbing the peace, he voluntarily stood trial at Truro and was acquitted by a packed jury, whereupon Cornwall declared for the King – one of very few counties to do so.

After Edgehill, a batch of commissions under the Great Seal was sent to Cornwall's isolated royalist commissioners. One of these, dated from Hampton Court on 14 November, empowered Sir Richard Vyvyan to erect one or more mints in the county to produce, from whatever bullion could be obtained, coinage of the prevailing designs and standards, to be delivered to Hopton, 'to whom we have given direction for the use of the same, for our service'. The commissioners forwarded this to Vyvyan on the 19th, instructing him to make his 'speedy repair' to them, suggesting Bodmin or Liskeard as suitable locations, and enclosed a declaration which enjoined 'all persons of what quallitie or degree soever' to bring in plate against satisfactory security and interest of eight per cent, 'which will be held the most acceptablest service can be done to his Majestie'.

Truro mint

Sir Richard Vyvyan of Trelowarren was MP for Tregony and head of one of Cornwall's oldest landed families (**4.1**). He was by now a prominent member of Cornwall's royalist command. Commissioned as Colonel of Foot for the Hundred of Powder on 1 August 1642, by mid-October his name appeared as one of the signatories on letters from the King's Cornish commissioners.

Fig. 4.1 Sir Richard Vyvyan, *c*.1643-4; attributed to William Dobson (1611-46). Dobson, described by Aubrey as 'the most excellent painter that England hath yet bred', lodged in Oxford throughout the war, where he produced many portraits of royalist officials. *Trelowarren, Cornwall, by courtesy of Sir Ferrers Vyvyan, Bt*

Vyvyan chose to set up his mint at Truro, a Stannary town and port, more convenient than Bodmin and more secure than Liskeard from the threat of raiding from Devon. Production seems to have started within a month or so, for by Christmas Vyvyan was reported to be too busy with his 'coyning of money' to attend to other duties, such as chasing up reluctant recruits. Our evidence for its location comes from Jonathan Rashleigh of Menabilly, one of the first to contribute plate, who took £104-worth to be melted for the King's service at 'Trewroe' and Abraham Biggs's undated account (late January 1643?) of costs of carriage of a trunk of plate seized from Lord Robartes of Lanhydrock 'to Trewrow to the mint'. Another unwilling contributor to the royalist war effort was a Plymouth merchant, Robert Trelawney from whom 681 oz of plate and a gold hatband weighing 3 oz were taken by Sir Nicholas Slanning on 14 January 1643.

A royalist victory at Braddock Down (19 January 1643) was followed by a serious reverse at Modbury, Devon (21 February); and although local truces bought time in February and March, hostilities were soon resumed. On 10 April 1643, Cornish royalists met at Bodmin, short of money and threatened with invasion from Parliament-held Devon. They decided to levy a weekly rate of £750 on the county and to raise a voluntary loan of plate. Lists of the plate gathered at Liskeard by 18 April and Killaton by the 24th, formerly at Mount Edgcumbe, near Plymouth, were unfortunately destroyed by an air raid in 1941, but Hopton's narrative tells us that £3,000-worth was brought in, probably including £101 from the recently-appointed Sheriff of the county, Francis Basset.

Hopton's army numbered only 2,400 foot and 500 horse, paid perhaps 8d and 2s 6d per day respectively. The ability to coin even £3,000, though small by comparison with the Tower Mint, may thus from a regional viewpoint be seen as an important contribution to the royalist campaign of 1643, since it provided significant help in fielding an army which against all the odds defeated a much larger and well-entrenched parliamentary force at Stratton, near Bude, on 16 May. The subsequent campaign was one of the great royalist successes of the war: almost the entire western peninsula was overrun (only Plymouth and Lyme Regis held out against them). It culminated in the battle of Roundway Down, near Devizes, on 13 July (see **3.13**), the capture of Bristol on 26 July and, finally that of Exeter on 4 September. Vyvyan's mint was soon on the move.

Exeter mint

A branch mint at Exeter had been planned by Parliament in December 1642, but was never opened (see. p.129). Technically, the royalist mint there dates from a commission issued to Vyvyan on 3 January 1644, which empowered him to set up one or more mints in the counties of Devon and Cornwall and city of Exeter (**4.2** and Appendix 1). However, two books detailing receipts and payments survive in the Vyvyan papers; covering the period 27 September 1643 to 2 April 1644, they show that the mint was set up almost immediately after Exeter was captured. In this time receipts of plate reckoned at 4s 10d per ounce of touched (hallmarked) gilt plate and 4s 8d for touched white plate amounted to £3,888 (the rates for untouched plate, of uncertain fineness, were 4s 2d and 4s 0d). Payments from the mint

Fig. 4.2 Commission, Sir Richard Vyvyan to erect a mint in Exeter, 3 January 1644. Vyvyan's second commission under the Great Seal; the text is transcribed in Appendix 1 on pp. 150-1. *Vyvyan papers, Cornwall Record Office V/BO/22a*

were £3,070. However, the books are incomplete (at least one page is missing) and not all receipts are recorded as fully paid in coin (see below); the figures are also complicated by a cash payment of £338, probably received in November. Copies of all receipts and other documents were kept by the mint's clerk, Thomas Hawkes, the only other member of staff who can be positively identified; it is sometimes suggested that Samuel Calle (or Cawley), for whom Vyvyan stood surety as a freeman of the city in 1645, may have been the engraver, though there is no certain evidence for this. The mint itself may have been located at the house belonging to Hannah Anthony, sister of parliamentarian goldsmith Edward Anthony, which Vyvyan occupied from 1643 until 1646, perhaps in St Olave's parish.

Exeter: a royalist mint at work

Documentary evidence for minting during the Civil War is very fragmentary. The two receipt books mentioned above provide a unique insight into the functioning of a Civil War mint and, as such, deserve our closer attention. They give us a lively picture of the day-to-day operation of a mint that served both as an arm of royalist military administration and the traditional function of a mint: a place where any citizen could bring bullion or manufactured plate for conversion into coinage. The books, marked on their covers 'A' and 'B', served different functions, though there is at first some overlap between them. Book B, entitled 'Acquittances for plate received for the King's use, Exon 27 Septem 1643', was used solely to record plate seized from Parliamentarians, lent by the well-disposed, or brought in by royalist officials 'for his Majesty's service' (**4.3**). Amongst the fourteen entries are consignments from the Mayor, Christopher Clarke (883 oz, 29 September), Nicholas Broking, merchant (200 oz, 30 Sept) and the goldsmiths Edward Anthony (1,706 oz, 14 October) and Ralph Herman (800 oz, 26 October) – parliamentarians all. Royalists signing acquittances included the brothers John and Richard Hunkyn of Liskeard, George Westcombe of Lindridge and Alan Penny, of whom more below. The 1,492 ounces received from John Bampfield of Poltimore on 3 November seem to have formed a (forced?) loan from a repentant rebel. Sir John Davie, baronet, of Sandford (197 oz, 8 January 1644) was a Parliamentary commissioner for Devon in 1642, but was ultimately to compound as a royalist 'delinquent' in 1646, fined £800, or one-tenth of his estate.

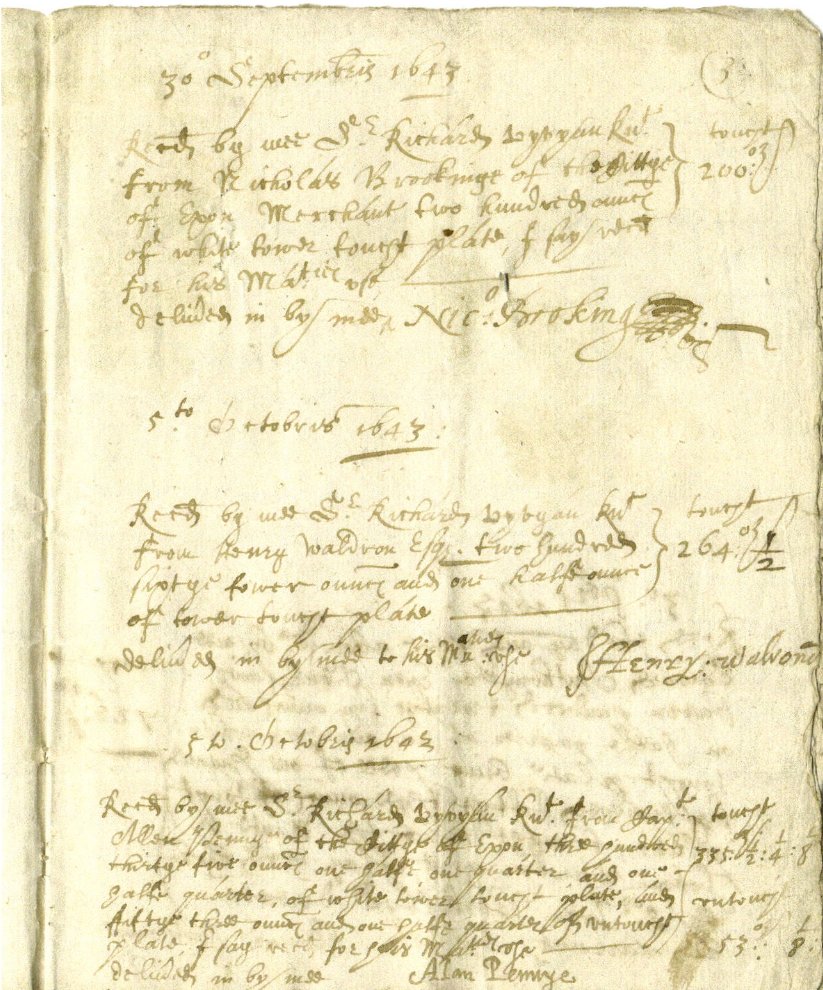

Fig. 4.3 Exeter mint accounts, book 'B', p.3: acquittances for plate delivered by Nicholas Broking on 30 September 1643 and by Henry Walrond and Captain Alan Penny on 5 October. *Vyvyan papers, Cornwall Record Office V/BO/20*

At the back of Book B, Vyvyan tabulated the values in sterling of the plate recorded in the acquittances. The first payment of coin was of £300 to Hugh Hodges, a Dorset attorney and deputy treasurer of the army, on 20 October, three weeks to the day from the first receipt of plate. Little new plate was recorded after early November. The summaries show that 5,100 oz of plate, valued at just under £1,200 were entered, which with a cash sum of £338 paid by Edward Anthony to redeem some of his plate came to £1,531; of this, £1,460 were paid out by early April 1644, mainly to Hodges (**4.4**).

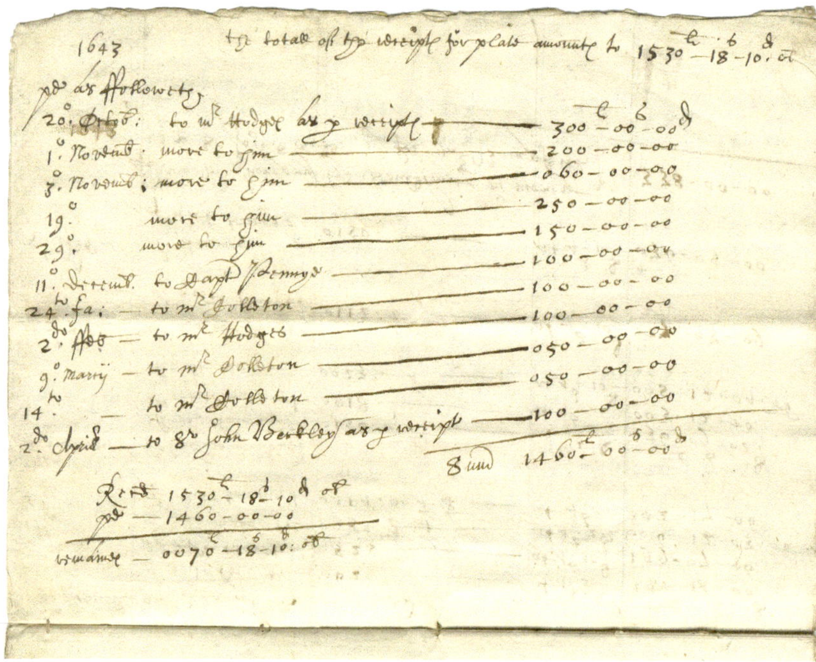
1643 the totall of the receipts for plate amounts to 1530–18–10 ob

pd as followeth

20 Octob: to mr Hodges as by receipt — 300–00–00

1 Novemb: more to him — 200–00–00

3 Novemb: more to him — 060–00–00

19 more to him — 250–00–00

29 more to him — 150–00–00

11 Decemb. — 100–00–00

24 — 100–00–00

2 — to mr Hodges — 100–00–00

9 — 050–00–00

14 — 050–00–00

2 April — to Sr John Berkley as by receipt — 100–00–00

Sum 1460–00–00

Rec 1530–18–10 ob

pd — 1460–00–00

remaines — 0070–18–10 ob

Fig. 4.4 Exeter mint accounts, book 'B': summary of payments to royalist officials, 20 October 1643 – 2 April 1644. *Vyvyan papers, Cornwall Record Office V/BO/20*

Book A, with 33 entries mostly in November and December 1643, served a somewhat different purpose: here are recorded deliveries of plate brought in, coined and returned to its owners (**4.5**). In this rôle it was used by royalist, parliamentarian and presumably neutral alike. The parliamentarian goldsmiths Edward Anthony and William Bartlett both brought in plate, as did another goldsmith, John Lavers. Lavers appears regularly, always bringing in substantial amounts of touched plate. It may be that he acted as a point of receipt for the mint; he was certainly a royalist and in 1646 compounded on the Exeter articles. Another regular visitor was Captain Alan Penny, an Exeter merchant who had been gaoled as a royalist troublemaker in December 1642. Released in 1643, he became a captain in the royal army, was to become Treasurer of the Western Association and commanded a company in Exeter in the final siege in 1645-6.

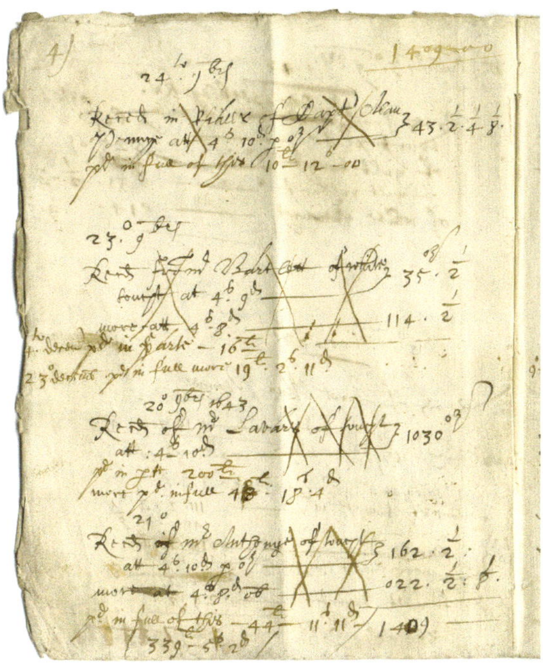

Fig. 4.5 Exeter mint accounts, book 'A', p.4: receipts and payments, November-December 1643. All are paid in full and cancelled. Note the receipt of 'rialls' from Alan Penny, 24 November. *Vyvyan papers, Cornwall Record Office V/BO/21*

It is hard to be sure, but plate appears to have been processed within about one week; receipt days were normally Saturdays and the Sabbath was strictly observed, except for one payment in Book B to Hodges. Vyvyan could not always pay on the spot and several part-payments are recorded; upon full payment, each entry was crossed through. Some, however, remained uncancelled. Two relating to Anthony may have been part of the basis of a post-war lawsuit against Vyvyan. Other intriguing entries include a consignment of over 2,800 oz, the biggest single entry, from Prince Maurice on 9 October: striking confirmation, perhaps of his reputation as a plunderer; this entry too is not cancelled and it is not certain the plate was coined. On 12 December Penny brought in 75 oz, a quarter of which was promptly returned and a further 20¼ oz (a single piece unmelted?) sent to the governor Sir John Berkeley's wife a week later. And why did Peter Sainthill MP of Bradninch, a royalist, deliver a parcel of plate on 1 December, only to take it all back again, apart from two flagons?

Few actual pieces of plate are mentioned; their weights and fineness were all that mattered. A consignment brought in on 18 November included a gilt basin weighing nearly 47 oz and a sugar dish of white touched plate weighing 19¾ oz; Sainthill's flagons weighed 101 oz between them. Vyvyan's rates were a little ungenerous measured against the Oxford rate of 5s for white touched plate (he was, after all, authorised to recover his operating costs without accounting for them) but to some extent negotiable, for allies such as Lavers, the merchant John Colleton and Robert Walker, MP for Exeter, even (on one occasion) Bartlett, were sometimes paid 4s 9d or even 4s 10d for touched white plate. Payments from the mint between October 1643 and early January 1644 recorded in Book A are £1,610. Taken with the figures from Book B and allowing for Anthony's cash, this gives a <u>minimum</u> output for the mint between September 1643 and early April 1644 of £2,732, nearly twice the figure usually quoted, which is based on Book B alone.

All bullion arriving at a mint was normally assayed and the correct final alloy obtained by blending different parcels. Several batches of 'ryalls' – Spanish silver dollars – would have been particularly useful here, for at around 94 per cent silver they were finer than sterling. These were a familiar sight in a port with strong continental trading connections: during the 1643 siege, the City Chamber offered to receive Spanish 'peeces of eight' at five shillings per ounce. Vyvyan, too, was prepared to pay a premium for them, offering 4s 9d or 4s 10d. The mint equipment included rings for making 'teasts' (bone ash cupels), suggesting that assays were indeed carried out at Exeter. Modern analyses indicate that the sterling standard was in general maintained. The coins themselves were manufactured by the traditional manual methods, much as described on p.16, above.

Truro and Exeter coinage

Vyvyan was instructed to produce money with 'the like stamp and forme as the moneys now current', and proceeded to do so. Unlike the 'Exurgat' coins, therefore, they at first bore no dates, though this changed in 1644; there has long been uncertainty as to the correct attribution of many of his products. Technique seems to have evolved from crude beginnings; the first half crowns, from a pair of dies that rapidly broke, bore as privy-mark a 'bugle horn' (**4.6**), perhaps a canting reference to *Cornubia* (Cornwall, the 'horn of Britain'). Thereafter, Vyvyan used a rose as his mark, through until 1645, when it was replaced by a tower or castle, perhaps derived from Exeter's arms, or the signature 'Ex'. At both mints half crowns formed the bulk of their output (e.g., **4.7**, **4.10**). Those attributable to Truro come from equal numbers of obverse and reverse dies, used more or less interchangeably. Thereafter, few obverse dies were used with many reverses – a technical change which might signify the move to a new mint at Exeter. Something similar is seen in the undated silver crowns: the first die pair (**4.8**) survives quite commonly, and might represent the coining of part of Hopton's £3,000 at Truro. The next pair of dies might belong to either

Fig. 4.6 Half crown, p.m. *Buglehorn, c*.1642. Very probably the first of Vyvyan's issues, from dies that quickly cracked and broke; the full design has been reconstructed from the few surviving specimens, none of which bears more than partial impressions. *Spink & Son Ltd/ drawing by Tony Daly*

Fig. 4.7 Half crown, Truro, 1642-3, p.m. Rose. The crisp engraving, partial impressions, and wrinkly shape are characteristic. It is sometimes suggested that the unusual T-shaped punctuation marks on the reverse were intended to represent the mint's initial.

Fig. 4.8 Crown, p.m. Rose, c.1643. This coin survives in considerable numbers and clearly formed one of Vyvyan's larger issues, probably part of the £3,000 coined at Truro in April-May 1643. *Spink & Son Ltd*

Fig. 4.9 Gold ten shillings, Truro, p.m. *Rose*, *c*.1643. The privy mark and form of the lettering make this the only gold coin that may with certainty be ascribed to Truro. *Courtesy of the Trustees of the British Museum*

Fig. 4.10 Half crown, Exeter, undated, *c*. late 1643/early 1644, p.m. *Rose*. The squarish shape and somewhat uneven striking is characteristic of the early Exeter products, when the mint was at its busiest.

mint, while the third obverse die was used with five different reverses. Most of what used to be called 'Truro or Exeter' must surely represent the high output of the first months at Exeter, covered by the two receipt books.

Both mints also produced gold – Truro presumably from the likes of Trelawney's hatband. A single surviving ten-shillings piece (**4.9**) may from its privy-mark and lettering be assigned to Truro. Several twenty-shillings gold pieces survive, all struck from the same obverse die, at Exeter (see below). Rare shillings may be attributed to Truro, while Exeter produced a full range of smaller denominations from shillings, sixpences down to a penny (**4.11**). There is in the British Museum a single silver ten shillings struck from crown dies, probably an early Exeter product.

Fig. 4.11 Penny, Exeter 1644, p.m. *Rose*; shilling, Exeter 1645, p.m. *Rose*.

Three pairs of dies which bear Vyvyan's privy-mark fall outside the remainder of the sequence: at some point he obtained dies for the gold 20s (**4.12**), silver half crowns (e.g. **4.13**) and shillings, which were certainly cut at the Oxford mint, in mid-late 1643; Vyvyan may have visited Oxford early in November (the Exeter mint books record no activity between the 4th and the 17th, suggesting that he was away) and he certainly attended the Oxford Parliament in January 1644.

Fig. 4.12 Gold twenty shillings, Exeter, *c*.1644-5, p.m. *Rose*. *Courtesy of the Trustees of the British Museum*

Fig. 4.13 Half crown, Exeter, dated 1644. The Oxford-made obverse die, to which he added his own privy-mark, was acquired by Vyvyan late in 1643 or early in 1644. This form of the mark continued in use beyond 25 March 1644, but was replaced soon afterwards by another rose mark, which we see here on the reverse.

Small numbers of half crowns and shillings of 'Exurgat' type were produced at Exeter in 1644 and 1645, perhaps to mark special events, though we cannot be sure what these were. Another puzzle is presented by a group of half crowns dated '1642', with an obverse die depicting the King galloping on horseback brandishing a scroll (**4.14**). Formerly thought to be Truro's first products, these well-made coins, from their position in the die cutting sequence, belong to Exeter in 1644 and may have been issued on two occasions. 'Galloping horse' dies were a feature of some of Truro's half crowns, but here the date must be commemorative, though again we cannot be sure of what. The inspiration for the design was probably the 'Scots Rebellion' medal of 1639 (**4.15**).

Fig. 4.14 Half crown, dated 1642. This unusual coin was issued on more than one occasion: there are two reverse dies, one with the 'Truro' rose as privy-mark, the other (seen here) the 'Exeter' rose. Both reverses were cut at Exeter and the obverse was used again with other reverses dated 1644 and 1645.

Fig. 4.15 The Scots rebellion, silver medal, London 1639. An early work by Thomas Simon.

Last days

Vyvyan spent most of the war in Exeter and in August 1644 took part in the King's campaign in Cornwall against the Earl of Essex. At Boconnoc on 3 September 1644 he was created baronet for his services to the royal cause, which included erecting and garrisoning a fort at Denis Head to guard the Helford river. Exeter was besieged in December 1645 and surrendered on 13 April 1646. There is no Exeter coinage dated 1646, while much of that dated 1645 (**4.16**) may well have been produced under siege late in the Old Style year, restricting its circulation. There is only one coin of that year in the late Civil War hoard found in 1895 at East Worlington, 19 miles (30 km) north of Exeter, which otherwise included a considerable batch of Vyvyan's products.

Fig. 4.16 Crown, Exeter 1645, with privy-marks *Castle* (obv.) and Ex (Rev.). A fine example of the idiosyncratic equestrian portraits of the Exeter series. The change of Privy-marks may signify that the mint was no longer in Vyvyan's hands, perhaps after his imprisonment by Berkeley during the final siege of the city.

Vyvyan spent the last weeks of the siege in prison, having fallen out with the governor, Sir John Berkeley, for speaking 'civilly' of Fairfax's army; Berkeley had his house searched and the mint records removed. Vyvyan was comprised within the Exeter articles of surrender, but faced immense local hostility. The mint tools, his personal property, were taken and in addition to compounding for his estates he faced a number of lawsuits concerning plate taken to the mint and for unlawfully occupying the Exeter house. Vyvyan was only able to clear these up by a costly, lengthy and resolute action, with powerful support from Sir Thomas Fairfax and other senior Parliamentary figures. Even so, he was not finally clear of litigation until July 1650. To these suits we owe the survival of the mint receipt books, retrieved from Berkeley, who had fled to France.

The list of tools taken from Vyvyan in 1646 throws some light on the mint, confirming traditional manual techniques. They include a box of small puncheons and tools, six upper and five under stamps (dies) 'not cutt' and twenty-three each of under and upper stamps, the distinction between them, even uncut, suggesting piles and trussels. There were also anvils, shears, tongs and hammers, and so on. The 'under stamps' represent most of those used in the entire Truro-Exeter series, while the upper stamps will have been those in use towards the end of the mint's life.

*****

There was a curious postscript to the West Country coinage. In the last months of the war there was a project to revive a mint at Truro under Col. William Smyth, which appears to have come to nothing. Smyth subsequently seems to have set up a mint on the island of Jersey, the destination of Prince Charles and other senior royalists in June 1646. A contemporary Jersey diarist, Jean Chevalier, recorded that half crowns, a few shillings and a good number of 'Jacobus' (gold unites of James I) were produced.

The half crowns were said to bear on one side the King on horseback with a sword in his hand and on the other 'the harp, roses (*plural*), fillets, interlaced crosses and other devices on the King's coin'; Chevalier later described the reverse as 'the same design as English coin'. The rather loose association of the words 'Truro' and 'roses' has led some writers to seek these coins in the Truro-Exeter series (privy-mark *a rose*), but this seems to me to be misguided. Perhaps the 'roses' were a misinterpretation of the scrolls of the garniture surrounding the shield on many Carolean half crowns.

The Jersey mint soon failed and appears to have been little better than a counterfeiting operation. None of its products, described by Sir Edward Hyde as 'adulterate' (i.e., light, base or both), has been identified. The Jersey mint was a far cry from Vyvyan's careful operation.

Chapter 5

YORK MINT

About the end of January [1643], the King's Mint began to coin in Sir Henry Jenkins House in the Minster Yard

York was Charles I's second capital, and after being forced to leave London he made his way there, arriving on 19 March 1642. Until the middle of August his court was based at York or Beverley, whence he directed operations against the port of Hull. The establishment of a mint at York was being planned long before the outbreak of formal hostilities. Nicholas Briot, the King's engraver, was summoned to York by a letter from Secretary of State Edward Nicholas dated 6 May in connection with some proposals concerning currency standards. A letter

Fig. 5.1 William Cavendish, successively Earl, Marquess (1643) and Duke (1665) of Newcastle. Nineteenth-century etching after Van Dyck.

of 30 May notes that Briot had fallen ill; it does not press him, but on 21 June, Secretary Nicholas ordered Briot to York forthwith 'et vous avertir qu'avez mener avec vous les Roues et toutes autres sortes d'instruments requis et necessaires pour icy battre de la Monnaye qu S. ma'té aura occasion d'ordonner dez que vous serez arrivé'. Shortly after, arrangements were made for Sir William Parkhurst, Warden of the Mint, to advance Briot the money necessary for his journey. On 15 July these plans received a severe setback when a ship carrying Briot's equipment and personal baggage was held up off Scarborough by one Captain Stevens, who seized the equipment on the grounds that no authority had been given for its removal. (Briot got his clothes back in August.) Meanwhile on 7 July, David Ramage, a member of Briot's staff, was paid £85 10s for the provision of 'several instruments for the two mints at York and Shrewsbury'.

In the meantime, the King was touring the north Midlands seeking men and supplies. He despatched a warrant establishing the mint at York, which arrived on the very day its equipment was taken. This we learn from a letter written the following day from Beverley, which was printed in London four days later:

Fig. 5.2 St William's College, otherwise 'Sir Henry Jenkins' house in the Minster Yard', site of the York mint, 1643-4. *E Besly*

> FRIDAY [*15 July*] a warrant under His Majestie's Broade Seale came to York for the erecting of a new Mynt there, some commissioners appointed for the same came to view the place, where the old Mynt stood, which is now in Sir William Saviles possession, near the Minster, where it appears money was coyned in Hen. 8 reigne.

The building referred to is St Leonard's Hospital which had housed a mint in 1546. However, August saw the removal of the Court as Charles set off to raise his standard at Nottingham and to recruit an army in the Welsh Marches. York became a military backwater, held by the Earl of Cumberland with a small garrison, and the need for large sums of money moved elsewhere.

In October William Cavendish, Earl of Newcastle and the wealthiest man in the north (**5.1**), was commissioned General of all forces to be raised in all parts of the kingdom 'Trent-north' and in many Midlands counties which were at that time in parliamentarian hands. He was also empowered to confer knighthoods and to coin money and print when he saw the occasion for it. In December he brought his forces to York, where a contemporary bewailed the lack of organization: officers and gentry had to dig deep into their pockets to provide for the army's upkeep. The mint finally started production in January 1643, not in St Leonard's Hospital, but in a building in Minster Yard, which today survives as St William's College and belongs to the Diocese of York (**5.2**). Christopher Hildyard's *Antiquities of York City*, first published in 1664, gives us our only reference to the mint in action, quoted above. He also tells us that the King's printers set up their presses there on 24 March 1642. All but one of them departed in the autumn of 1642, releasing suitable accommodation for the mint.

Four silver denominations were produced at York: half crowns (**5.3**, **5.5**), shillings (**5.4**, **5.6**), sixpences (**5.6**) and threepences (**5.4**). Its coins were highly unusual for the time on account of the quality of the die-engraving and perfection of the printed image – an apt term, perhaps, since they were produced on a rotary press. Strips of silver were prepared and fed between pairs of steel rollers mounted in a machine like a mangle, operated, if Briot's earlier experiments are a guide, by two 'strong persons'. Each roller bore a series of engraved dies (five or six for half crowns, shillings and sixpences, nine for the threepences) and the coins were punched out afterwards, a process which might give a bowed profile and could leave a burred edge on the reverse of the coin (e.g., the shilling **5.4**), which in extreme cases was filed flat. Almost all York coins are identified by the mint-signature EBOR (*Eboracum*, the Latin name of the city) and all use a lion, an element of the city's arms, as a privy mark (**5.3**). At their best, York's coins are the finest-looking English coinage of the time. All too often, however, the coining machine was poorly adjusted, the metal was insufficiently annealed, or the cutter-punch gave trouble and the coins bear incomplete or uneven images.

Fig. 5.3 Half crown, York *c*.1643, p.m. *Lion*. The privy-mark, method of production and find spots identify this as a York coin. Teething trouble with the cutter punch may explain why many of these coins were crudely cut from the strip using shears.

Fig. 5.4 York threepence and shilling, *c*.1643, signed EBOR (*Eboracum*). More early products, like 5.3 the work of an unknown engraver.

Fig. 5.5 Half crown, York 1643-4, signed EBOR, showing the incomparable clarity of a coin produced by rotary methods. The horseman copies Tower half crowns of 1642-3 (10.1). *Penybryn Treasure Trove*

Fig. 5.6 York shilling (EBOR) and sixpence, p.m. *Lion*, 1643-4, with characteristic portraits by Briot.

There also exist several types of 'York' half crowns which do not fit into this scheme. One issue comprises two 'York' types and two which copy Tower issues of 1639-41, using dies made from a single set of punches. All are highly debased (as low as 44% silver) using as alloy copper whitened with arsenic, a standard contemporary counterfeiting recipe, and are of very low weight, giving intrinsic values around ten pence, i.e., one third of their face value. Nowhere did the royalists debase by this much. An example of a 'Tower' type in the 1985 Breckenbrough hoard shows them to be contemporary, and the coins are well made, but it is hard to think of them other than as counterfeits. Another small group of lightweight half crowns copies York types, but in good silver. It is also contemporary (one has been excavated at Sandal Castle, demolished in 1646) but its status remains uncertain.

Newcastle delegated the day-to-day running of the mint to a local lawyer, William Martin, 'gent & attorney'. Like Vyvyan, Martin was a thoroughly modern multi-tasking operator, who also manufactured pistols for the royalists. There appears to be no other written evidence for the names of any of York's officials. Experienced staff may have been recruited from Edinburgh, where Briot's machines were in use. The active involvement of Nicholas Briot at York is testified by his correspondence of 1642, his widow Esther's petition to Charles II ('he from time to time did go to York'), the use of rotary coining machinery and the engraving of some of the dies (**5.6**). His pupil David Ramage, a competent if uninspired engraver, may have been responsible for the dies for the first group of half crowns (**5.3**) and we may note that the portraits on the threepences and on one group of shillings (**5.4**), which were probably early products, lack Briot's refinement and may be by another, unidentified engraver.

Apart from what the coins tell us, we know very little about the operation of Martin's mint; like Exeter, it probably also served the local community. One of its clients may have been the city's Corporation, which in February 1644, desperately short of ready money, approved the sale of £100-worth of the City's plate. Like Exeter College, Oxford (see Chapter 3), the Corporation recorded this plate: basins, ewers, bowls, salts and 'levery potts', together with their weights and donors. It seems highly likely that these were converted into coinage.

The mint's potential importance to the royalists lay not only in the converting of plate, but also in the recoinage of foreign specie. Until Bristol was captured, the north-eastern ports were a vital channel of supplies from Europe. On 7 March 1643, for instance, the Queen arrived at York from the Netherlands bringing supplies rumoured to include large amounts of coin (see below, Chapter 7). York's products were used locally, for instance in purchasing foodstuffs. They have been recorded in at least thirteen hoards from Yorkshire and neighbouring counties, notably those from Breckenbrough, near Thirsk, discovered in 1985, Grewelthorpe, North Yorkshire (1991) and Pocklington, east of York, found in 1848 – a major source of fresh coins from the mint. The mint remained active until the spring of 1644, when York was besieged by the joint armies of Lord Fairfax, the Scots and the Eastern Association. The siege was raised, brilliantly, by Prince Rupert on 1 July, but the royalist disaster at Marston Moor the following day led swiftly to a new siege which a much-reduced garrison was unable to withstand. Articles for the city's surrender were agreed on15 July 1644.

Chapter 6

SIR THOMAS CARY'S MINTS

W.H. Black's *Docquets of Letters Patent and Other Instruments passed under the Great Seal of King Charles I at Oxford*, published in 1837, includes on p.211 the following entry (22 May 1644):

> A commission directed to Sr Thomas Cary Kt whereby his Maty doth authorize him to erect one or more mynts within the Counties of Hereford Worcester Salop and Chester and to Coyne moneyes in such manner as in the Tower of London, And to receive for his Paynes and Chardges in coyning the said moneyes such Allowances as are paid in the said Tower of London without Accompt and to paie so much of the said Moneys as shalbe made of the Ingott Bullion or Plate delivered to his Mats use, to Prince Rupert or such as he shall appointe.

The task of identifying Sir Thomas 'Cary' is not helped by a profusion of Thomas Car(e)ys and Thomas Carews who lived during Charles I's reign. One, the younger brother of the second Earl of Monmouth, is the Thomas Cary, Gentleman of the King's Bedchamber, depicted on a medal by the French engraver Warin in 1633. It has been stated, erroneously, that he served the King during the Civil War and died late in Old Style 1648; in fact he died (seemingly of consumption) as Ambassador-designate to Venice in April 1634 and must therefore be ruled out as a royalist mint master. The only recorded *knight* of this name living in 1644 was the second son of Walter Cary, of Wickham, Bedfordshire; he had been dubbed in Ireland on 10 June 1628.

The commission to supply the border counties with mints appears at first to be an afterthought, but we know that there had been plans to reopen the mint at Shrewsbury in the summer of 1643, which had been shelved after the capture of Bristol. It may have stemmed, ultimately, from the appointment in January 1644 of Prince Rupert as Captain-General in the Welsh Marches. Among reforms that he introduced was an overhaul of local taxation; henceforth, taxes could be paid in kind, which presumably might include plate and thereby create a need for local mints related to the tax-gathering centres. Mints are known to have existed at Chester and Hereford, though surviving coins can be securely attributed only to the former. A document giving details of 277 ounces of plate coined at Hereford by 'Rude the coyner' in October-November 1644 was published in 1898 but cannot now be found; he coined at 5s per ounce and was paid 4d per ounce for his pains. The date and place together suggest that one of Cary's mints is concerned. No other mints or coins can be attributed with certainty, but there is a considerable series of coins from Chester, from another significant royalist mint or mints and several small issues of half crowns; these coins appear in hoards deposited in 1644 or later and occasionally as isolated finds. The find spots indicate origins in Wales or the Marches rather than south-west England, the other main area to which the royalists became increasingly restricted in the later stages of the war. These coins are likely to be the products of Cary's mints.

Chester mint

Chester was garrisoned for the King from September 1642 and remained in royalist hands almost to the end, surrendering on 3 February 1646. It is possible that a mint may have operated there as early as December 1643, but the evidence is inconclusive. The Mayor and Aldermen of the city offered 400 oz of gilt plate (about £100-worth) to Arthur, Lord Capel, as a bribe for the removal of the newly-arrived troops from Ireland. Capel's receipt of 7 December refers to the plate as an 'advance or contribution to the pay and provision of and for the fforces arrived from Ireland and now in his Majesty's service in thes parts', but we do not know if it was coined; on 16 December the same quantity was signed for, on the same receipt, by Brian

Pretious, a local man. Its ultimate fate is unknown: the survival of the plate for at least nine days might argue against the existence of a functioning mint at this point. A mint was certainly working by 31 January 1645, when it was ordered that £100-worth of the city's remaining plate be 'fourthwith converted into coyne' towards the city's defence and payment of its debts. One securely identified Chester half crown (**6.1**) bears the date 1644, i.e. it was struck before 25 March 1645. This and a second type (**6.2**) bear as privy-marks the ancient armorials of the city, three gerbs (wheatsheaves) together with the upright sword granted as the crest of the city's new arms in 1580, best seen here on **6.2**, which is also signed CHST. An exceedingly rare gold twenty shillings (**6.3**) is linked to these by the use of the same punches in preparing its dies and so should also be ascribed to Chester. It was formerly thought to have been produced at Aberystwyth, even though coining in gold lay outside the terms of Thomas Bushell's indentures.

Fig. 6.1 Half crown of *Exurgat* type, Chester 1644, privy-marks *Three gerbs and a sword* (obv.), *Feathers* (rev.).

Fig. 6.2 Chester half crown, undated, with p.m. *three gerbs and a sword* on both sides, the obverse signed CHST below the horse. Apparently from the same obverse die as 6.1, crudely recut with the addition of feathers and the mint signature.

Fig. 6.3 Gold twenty shillings, undated, p.m. *Feathers*. Attributed to Chester by the identity of the feathers and other punches to those used for the dies of 6.1 and 6.2.

Two further types, a half crown and a threepence, bear a single prostrate gerb as privy-mark (**6.4**). All of these coins are linked by their mode of manufacture using a rotary (rocker) press but, apart from the dated type, their chronology is uncertain. There are other half crowns and shillings, also made by this method, the designs of which suggest a relationship to Chester – if not actual production there (**6.5**, **6.6**). The designs of these coins (note, for instance the lionskin garniture on the reverse of **6.5**) and the use of a rotary technique raise the possibility that staff from the York mint provided technical support for the establishment and operation of the mint at Chester but, again, we are unable at present to say whether this was before or after York's surrender (15 July 1644).

Fig. 6.4 Half crown and threepence, p.m. *a single gerb*, probably struck at Chester. The reverse of the half crown is similar to York coins 5.5 – 5.6.

Fig. 6.5 Half crown with privy-marks *three pellets*, one of two specimens from the Penybryn hoard. The find spot, only fifteen miles away, and similarity to 6.4 point to a Chester origin. *Penybryn Treasure Trove*

Fig. 6.6 Shilling, p.m. three pellets, uncertain mint (Chester?)

Worcester and related issues

The largest of Cary's issues was for many years attributed to a completely different part of England – the so-called Weymouth and Salisbury series, a factoid that once ensconced in numismatic literature has proved remarkably hard to shift, despite a complete lack of evidence for any minting, let alone by the royalists, at either place and an equally comprehensive lack of local finds. The group comprises an extensive series of half crowns bearing a variety of privy-marks and linked by the use of common punches and dies; a series of related smaller denominations, from shillings down to half groats; and some very rare gold twenty-shillings pieces. With one exception, these coins bear designs related to Tower Mint issues, as required by Cary's commission. The exception is the half crown that heads the sequence, an 'Exurgat' issue dated 1644, the reverse die for which was first used – dated 1643 – at Bristol: another example, perhaps, of co-operation and support for a new mint from a well-established one.

The first two half crown obverse dies of this series bear a letter W beneath the King's horse and in keeping with royalist practice after 1643 this is likely to identify their place of minting, however obscurely (**6.7**). Reference to the far-from-specific armorial charges used as privy-marks led numismatists to attribute the coins to Weymouth, but there is no record of any grant for a mint in Dorset; indeed, as George Boon pointed out, the royalist ordnance agent in Weymouth, Captain Strachan, was forever complaining about shortage of cash. On the other hand, a West Midlands source is suggested by finds from Flintshire, Wrexham, Shropshire and the Cotswolds as well as finds from south and west Wales. Some shillings bear a privy-mark that resembles a pear, an element of the arms of Worcester (*Wigornia*), *Civitas in Bello et Pace fidelis*, held for the King until 23 July 1646 and which seems most likely to have been the site of Sir Thomas Cary's principal mint.

Fig. 6.7 Half crown, signed W (Worcester?) with privy-marks [*Castle*] (here illegible) and *Helmet, c.* 1644-5. *Penybryn Treasure Trove*

Another half crown die bears the letters SA and it has been suggested that these signify *Salopia*, the Latin name for Shrewsbury (**6.8**). The letters marking the origins of the major royalist series – OX, BR, EX, W – could all in principle represent Latin names, but only at York (EBOR) is this explicit. In July 1643, Thomas Bushell's plans to reopen the mint at Shrewsbury had progressed as far as sending men to prepare the furnaces, so this type may represent an issue at Shrewsbury as one of Cary's mints between May 1644 and 22 February 1645, when the town was surprised and captured. There are two find spots for SA half crowns, both near Haverfordwest in Pembrokeshire; these, perhaps, could represent money brought in to that area by the repeated raids by Sir Charles Gerard from the Marches deep into Wales in April and May 1645 and do not of themselves negate Shrewsbury as their place of origin.

Fig. 6.8 Half crown, signed SA (*Salopia*?), with privy-marks *Fleur-de-lys* and [*Scallop*], *c*. 1644-5. The crude production is characteristic of many coins in the Cary series. *Tregwynt Treasure Trove*

Fig. 6.9 Shilling, p.m. Pear (?), Cary series, *c*. 1644-5; threepence, p.m. *Fleur-de-lys*, Cary series, *c*. 1644-5.

Like Chester, the W/SA mint(s) produced a full range of denominations; there are extremely rare gold twenty-shillings pieces and silver from half crowns and shillings (**6.9**) down to a half groat. The SA die was used again, some time in 1645, presumably, with these letters obliterated by a roundel ('cannon ball'), presumably at a different site (**6.10**). Half crowns from this and later dies in the sequence have been found in Shropshire and Flintshire, while a threepence of related type came to light in 1989 in the Vale of Glamorgan and a half groat has been found near Gloucester. The coins at the very end of the sequence are noticeably debased, to judge from their appearance and this has been confirmed by modern analyses.

Fig. 6.10 Half crown, '**Salopia**' obverse with signature obliterated ('cannon ball'). Uncertain mint, *c.* 1645.

'Hartlebury Castle' and other related types

Hartlebury Castle, residence of the Bishop of Worcester, lies about ten miles north of that city and in 1644-5, like Worcester, was one of the collection centres for local taxes, the 'contribution'. There is a group of half crowns, all from a single pair of dies, with privy-marks (one and three pears) that leave little doubt of their Worcestershire origin (**6.11**). Hidden in the lower part of the garniture of the reverse shield are the letters H – C and, if these identify the mint, the suggestion of Hartlebury Castle is almost certainly correct. Specimens have occurred in hoards of 1644-6 in the Cotswolds and Shropshire, while an isolated example was found at Hanbury in Worcestershire. Hartlebury Castle was held by the royalists until 16 May 1646. A third Worcestershire centre for collection of the 'contribution' was at Evesham, lost on 26 May 1645. W.A. Cotton, in his *The Coins, Tokens and Medals of Worcestershire* (1885) refers on p.37 to a local tradition of a Civil War mint there, but there is apparently no corroborative evidence; a house in Bridge Street was known as 'The Mint' and Cotton was shown a half crown, '...but as it bore the m.m. (P), it was made at the Tower and evidently has no connection whatever with Evesham, except that it was unearthed in the neighbourhood'.

Fig. 6.11 Half crown, privy-marks *One pear* and *Three pears*, signed H – C in lower reverse garniture (barely legible here); probably Hartlebury Castle, 1644-6. This coin, from the collection of Sir Charles Oman, was probably part of the 'Cotswolds' hoard, found in around 1900.

The 'Hartlebury' coins were produced on a simple rotary (rocker) press and there are two other unattributed half crown issues which were made in the same way. The first (**6.12**) is dated 1644 and bears the initials CH; four specimens are known to survive, with two reverse dies and the only recorded find spot is Penybryn, near Ruabon, Wrexham. The second, also dated 1644, is of Exurgat type copying a Bristol original. One example (**6.13**) may have been included in the 'Cotswold' hoard buried in 1645; another was reportedly found near Grosmont, Monmouthshire, in around 2016. Their crude appearance notwithstanding, both are issues of good silver and full weight and they should be regarded as official royalist issues from the Welsh Marches. An attribution of either coin to Hereford (*Civitas Herefordiae*, in keeping with other Latin mint-names?) is not out of the question – but would be speculative. Attempts to link CH to 'Compton House' (Compton Wynyates, Warwickshire) and HC to Hawarden Castle (Flintshire) appear to me to be complete guesswork and serve only to muddy the waters.

Fig. 6.12 Half crown, dated 1644 and signed CH (Hereford?). The date, barely legible at the top of the reverse, is confirmed by the other surviving examples. *Penybryn Treasure Trove*

Fig. 6.13 Half crown of *Exurgat* type, uncertain mint, 1644. The 'Declaration' follows the form used on Bristol coins from 1643, which hints at a western origin for this type; the production by 'rocker press' suggests that it may form part of the Cary series.

The final half crown in this section remains a puzzle. A competent, if unremarkable equestrian obverse is coupled with a reverse of vigour and originality on which the crowned royal arms are surrounded by the ribbon of the Garter and supported by a lion and a unicorn (**6.14**). One specimen, in the British Museum, is undated, but all others bear the date 1645. The (unique?) undated coin is of fine silver but the 1645 coins are all somewhat debased (analyses suggest about 70-75% silver), a feature shared with some of the latest of the W/SA group discussed above. A woodcut of the 1645 half crown appears in Elias Ashmole's *The Institution, Laws & Ceremonies of the Noble Order of the Garter* published in 1672. According to Ashmole,

> … there were *an*. 21 *Car*. I certain half crowns stamped in the West of *England*, having the *Soveraign's Arms* so encompassed, and this was the first Money, whereon the Royal *Garter* appeared amongst us.

Ashmole had served the royalists as Commissioner of the Excise in various places, including Worcester, so it is likely that this curious issue also belongs in this region.

Fig. 6.14 Half crown, p.m. *Fleur-de-lys*, uncertain mint, 1645; reverse, royal arms with Garter, crown and supporters.

Chapter 7

FOREIGN COIN

In the normal course of events, any foreign coins entering the country were sent to the mint to be melted and reminted. They were generally excluded from circulation, though specific types were officially allowed from time to time, often in special circumstances (see p.11). Nevertheless, foreign coins were familiar sights in ports with trading connections, for instance coins from the Low Countries in East Anglian ports and Iberian coins in Exeter. In March 1639, the Exeter merchant John Hayne exchanged a quantity of 'Portugall testons' with 'Mr Harman the goldesmith'; the following month, Hayne exchanged 1,971 'rialls which came from Mr Budley of Dartmouth' with 'Mr Bartlet the goldesmith' (we have met Herman and Bartlett already [p.68, 71]). However, English hoards of the Stuart period very rarely contain European coins, with the noticeable exception of those of the 1640s. Does this reflect a contrast between hoarding habits in peacetime and those in a time of unrest? Or was there a genuine increase in the presence of foreign currency during the Civil War? Because the war accounts for the overwhelming majority of seventeenth-century hoards, it is hard to be sure, but I believe that this increase in foreign coinage was indeed a wartime phenomenon.

One special cause of this may have been royalist fund-raising on the Continent, especially in the Low Countries. On 23 February 1642, Queen Henrietta Maria left Dover for the Continent, to raise money for the King by pledging her own and some of the Crown Jewels. The high rate of interest she was charged (12%) was met from profits on the sale of Cornish tin in French and Flemish ports. Much of the borrowed money went to buy arms and equipment, but some arrived in England as specie. Early in the war, Thomas Bushell bore the cost of converting 'dollars' used for soldiers' pay; and the Earl of Newcastle is recorded as having received in October 1642, at Newcastle, a 'little barrel of ducatoons', amounting to £500 sterling, in one of the Queen's arms shipments from Holland. With no mint at that stage to recoin them, he may have distributed them as such. In due course, the advent of troops from Ireland and Scotland, both countries where European coins played a significant role, may also have brought foreign specie to England. Prize goods were another possible source, such as the five barrels of dollars, bound for merchants in Exeter, which were included amongst goods seized by Parliament's Lord Admiral, the Earl of Warwick, in June 1644.

A proclamation issued by the royalist administration in Oxford on 4 March 1644 made a number of foreign coin types legal tender at rates very close to their intrinsic values (**7.1** and Table IV), ostensibly for 'the advancement and quickning of trade in these distracted times' and probably in tacit recognition of their existing place in the currency.

Table IV: *Proclaimed and intrinsic values of foreign coin, 1644*

	Oxford Proclamation, March 1644	Tower Mint assays, January 1651 (value as coins)
SILVER		
Ducaton	5s 6d	5s 6⅛d
Rix Doller	4s 8d	4s 7¾d
Crosse Dollar	4s 6d	4s 4¾d
Piece of Eight	4s 6d	4s 6½d
Cardecue	1s 6d	1s 7d
GOLD		
Double Ryder	£1 1s 6d	£1 1s 11½d
Double Pistoll	£0 15s 0d	£0 14s 8⅔d

Of the gold types in the Oxford proclamation, a half-rider (*cf.* **7.2**) was included in a hoard found at Newark and Spanish double-escudos ('double pistolls', *cf.* **7.3**) have been found in Lincolnshire and Glamorgan. In silver, there are few records of Spanish (**7.4**) or Spanish-American eight-real pieces (the Middleham hoard included a couple and three counterfeits) and none (in a Civil War context) of cardecues or German Reichstaler ('Rix Dollars').

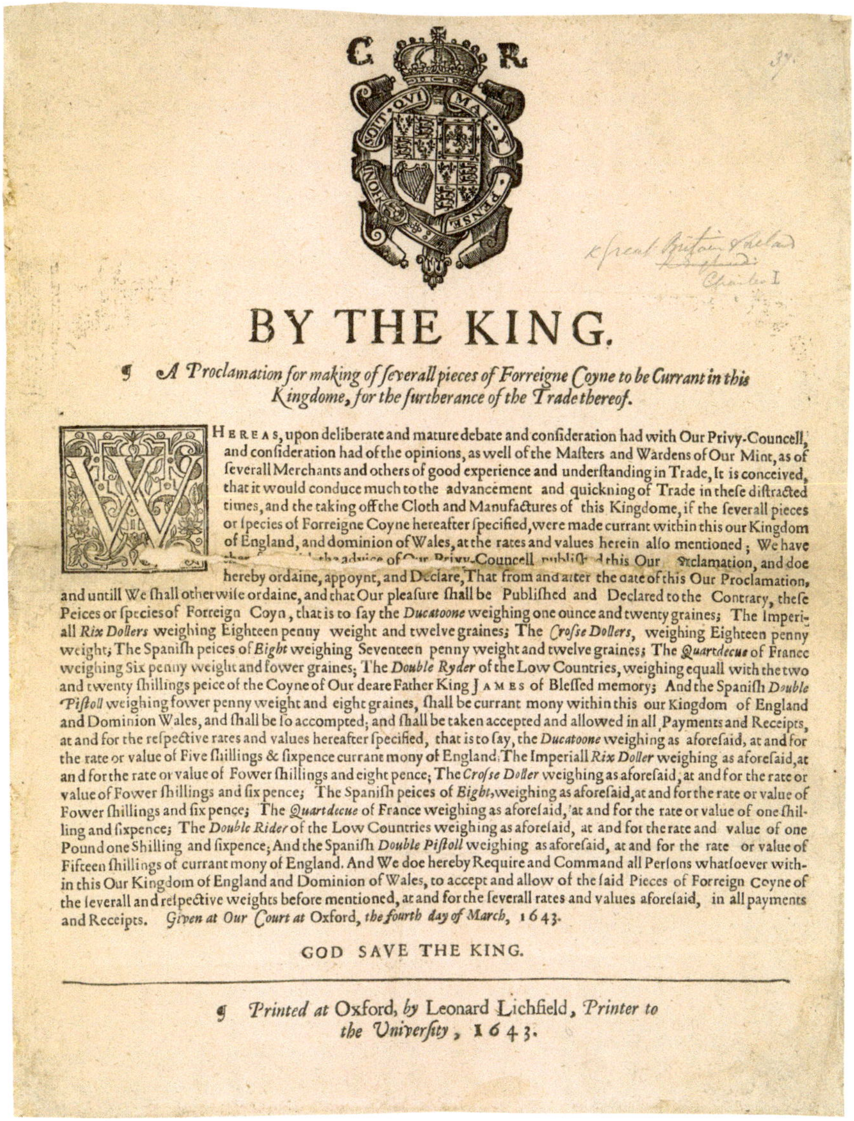

C R

BY THE KING.

¶ *A Proclamation for making of ſeverall pieces of Forreigne Coyne to be Currant in this Kingdome, for the furtherance of the Trade thereof.*

WHEREAS, upon deliberate and mature debate and conſideration had with Our Privy-Councell, and conſideration had of the opinions, as well of the Maſters and Wardens of Our Mint, as of ſeverall Merchants and others of good experience and underſtanding in Trade, It is conceived, that it would conduce much to the advancement and quickning of Trade in theſe diſtracted times, and the taking off the Cloth and Manufactures of this Kingdome, if the ſeverall pieces or ſpecies of Forreigne Coyne hereafter ſpecified, were made currant within this our Kingdom of England, and dominion of Wales, at the rates and values herein alſo mentioned; We have [illegible] the advice of Our Privy-Councell publiſhed this Our Proclamation, and doe hereby ordaine, appoynt, and Declare, That from and after the date of this Our Proclamation, and untill We ſhall otherwiſe ordaine, and that Our pleaſure ſhall be Publiſhed and Declared to the Contrary, theſe Peices or ſpecies of Forreign Coyn, that is to ſay the *Ducatoone* weighing one ounce and twenty graines; The Imperiall *Rix Dollers* weighing Eighteen penny weight and twelve graines; The *Croſse Dollers*, weighing Eighteen penny weight; The Spaniſh peices of *Eight* weighing Seventeen penny weight and twelve graines; The *Quartdecue* of France weighing Six penny weight and fower graines; The *Double Ryder* of the Low Countries, weighing equall with the two and twenty ſhillings peice of the Coyne of Our deare Father King JAMES of Bleſſed memory; And the Spaniſh *Double Piſtoll* weighing fower penny weight and eight graines, ſhall be currant mony within this our Kingdom of England and Dominion Wales, and ſhall be ſo accompted; and ſhall be taken accepted and allowed in all Payments and Receipts, at and for the reſpective rates and values hereafter ſpecified, that is to ſay, the *Ducatoone* weighing as aforeſaid, at and for the rate or value of Five ſhillings & ſixpence currant mony of England; The Imperiall *Rix Doller* weighing as aforeſaid, at and for the rate or value of Fower ſhillings and eight pence; The *Croſse Doller* weighing as aforeſaid, at and for the rate or value of Fower ſhillings and ſix pence; The Spaniſh peices of *Eight*, weighing as aforeſaid, at and for the rate or value of Fower ſhillings and ſix pence; The *Quartdecue* of France weighing as aforeſaid, at and for the rate or value of one ſhilling and ſixpence; The *Double Rider* of the Low Countries weighing as aforeſaid, at and for the rate and value of one Pound one Shilling and ſixpence; And the Spaniſh *Double Piſtoll* weighing as aforeſaid, at and for the rate or value of Fifteen ſhillings of currant mony of England. And We doe hereby Require and Command all Perſons whatſoever within this Our Kingdom of England and Dominion of Wales, to accept and allow of the ſaid Pieces of Forreign Coyne of the ſeverall and reſpective weights before mentioned, at and for the ſeverall rates and values aforeſaid, in all payments and Receipts. *Given at Our Court at* Oxford, *the fourth day of March*, 1643.

GOD SAVE THE KING.

¶ *Printed at* Oxford, *by* Leonard Lichfield, *Printer to the Univerſity*, 1643.

Fig. 7.1 Charles I, proclamation regarding the currency of foreign coins, Oxford, 4 March 1644. *British Library 1851.b.3 (37)*

Fig. 7.2 United Netherlands, Province of Utrecht, gold grote gouden rijder, 1617. Current in England and Wales at £1 1s 6d.

Fig. 7.3 Spain, Philip IV (1621-65), gold 2-escudos, Seville 1621. Current for 15s. These crudely-made 'cobs' rarely display more than a portion of their designs.

Fig. 7.4 Spain, Philip III (1598-1621), silver 8-reales, Segovia 1614; produced using a rotary press (compare the York coins in Ch. 5). Current for 4s 6d

Ducatons (**7.5**) and patagons ('Crosse Dollars', **7.6**) are by far the most commonly found of these foreign coin types. They turn up in hoards from Yorkshire, Lancashire, the Newark area and south Midlands, even in some West Country hoards, and occasionally as stray finds. There is an intriguing connection, perhaps, between many of these hoards and the itinerary pursued by the Queen in 1643 bearing, as was widely believed, large quantities of supplies from the Continent and, according to rumours that reached the Venetian ambassador in London, large sums of money. (Agostini believed her to have brought £80,000 in specie.) Her route took her from her landfall at Bridlington (22 February) to York (6 March), where she stayed until late May, via Doncaster, Newark (16 June – 3 July) and onward to her reunion with the King on the field of Edgehill on 13 July. Ducatons and/or patagons have been found in ten Yorkshire hoards and three from Nottinghamshire, amongst others, as well as a find from Broughton, Oxfordshire, very close to Wroxton, where the royal couple spent the night of 13 July 1643. Disbursements en route by the Queen's entourage might have provided one mechanism whereby some of these foreign coins entered circulation in royalist-held areas. In 1644 the Queen left again for the Continent via Exeter; at least two Devon hoards of that year, from Buckfastleigh and Totnes, have contained ducatons, and a quarter-patagon has been found at Wiveliscombe in west Somerset.

Fig. 7.5 Spanish Netherlands, Brabant, Philip IV (1621-65), silver ducaton, Antwerp (mint-signature, a hand) 1634. Current for 5s 6d.

One other small 'foreigner' perhaps deserves to be mentioned: the Scottish twenty-pence piece (**7.7**). This little coin is found widely in England and Wales, including in secure Civil-War contexts, such as the northern castles of Beeston (Cheshire) and Sandal, near Wakefield (South Yorkshire) and in the Wyke (Bradford) hoard. Equivalent to 1⅔d, these had no obvious place

Fig. 7.6 Spanish Netherlands, Brabant, Albert and Isabella (1598-1621), silver patagon, Antwerp 1619. Current for 4s 6d..

in English circulation, but probably passed as half groats (2d); often, they are counterfeit. There is a reference to losses relating to twopences that are 'not current' in Sir William Brereton's account book (Cheshire area); and in March 1645 the Parliamentary Committee in Staffordshire ordered John Wagge and William Hackney to satisfy a debt to Thomas Wyrley of Penkridge in 'good and lawful money' after Wyrley had been unable to 'put off' (exchange) the twopences 'being not current money' with which they had purchased 'certen apples' from him the previous November. These formed the subject of an enquiry to the Seaby *Bulletin* in July 1955, which apparently went unanswered at the time. It appears to me that the Scottish twenty-pences would fit the bill nicely as the 'two pences' in question – a parallel, perhaps, to the Venetian 'galyhalpens' of the fifteenth and sixteenth centuries, which circulated all over England and Wales at a rate well in excess of their intrinsic value and caused the authorities no end of bother. Whether the presence of the Scottish twenty-pence pieces relates to the arrival of the Scottish army in northern England early in 1644, the Scottish war of 1640, or whether these coins were simply an endemic nuisance, is another matter.

Fig. 7.7 Scotland, Charles I, silver twenty-pence piece, Third Coinage of 1637-42.

Chapter 8

SIEGE COINAGES OF THE CIVIL WAR

Towards the end of the war, many towns and castles in royalist hands had become isolated. In the artificial conditions within a besieged stronghold, there was often no need for money. At Lathom House, the Lancashire seat defended by the Countess of Derby, for instance:

> There was amongst the soldiers about fifty pounds in money, but of no use at all to them but to play at span-counter with: they lent to one another by handfuls, never telling nor counting any: one day one soldier had all, and the next another, 'till at last all their sport was spoiled, the enemy at the gate stript them of every penny and turned them out to the wide world.

During the siege of York there was an efficient system of free billeting, charged to the officers and gentry. Several besieged cities had mints anyway: York, Chester, Bristol, Exeter, Oxford. In a few cases, however, 'money of necessity' was coined. It was no novelty: the idea of siege money will have been familiar to those who had served in the European wars of the preceding decades. Such issues were produced by local governors acting on their own authority and are characterised by simple designs and often by unusual shapes and weight standards.

During 1645-6 three garrisons issued their own coins: Carlisle, Scarborough and Newark. What did these sieges have in common? Essentially they were lengthy affairs, of nine, eleven and six months respectively (in Newark's case its third siege in as many years). They involved the defence of towns and some attempts were made to maintain normal life. At Carlisle and Scarborough, it is clear that plate was coined only when money ran out. There is also in each case at least one contemporary and unambiguous reference to the production of these coinages.

The evidence from Scarborough (see below) makes clear the purpose of siege coinages: they were to pay the garrison – including the officers, and specifically for the labour of repairing the frequent breaches of the defences – when conventional sources of cash finally dried up. We should remember that from the outset loyalty was to a large degree conditioned by ability to pay. John Aubrey quotes the polyglot Croatian, Carlo Fantom, who served each side in turn: 'Said he, I care not for your cause: I come to fight for your half-crowne, and your handsome women.' (He was hanged, eventually, for 'ravishing'.) Late in the war, with the royalist cause increasingly obviously lost, what else would tempt the average soldier to fight on? While the officers and gentry had a lot to lose upon surrender, the rank and file usually either joined the successful besiegers, or were simply allowed to go home, having sworn not to take up arms again. While it lasted, military service was better paid than everyday labour.

Carlisle mint

In the wake of the battle of Marston Moor, Carlisle became an isolated outpost in the far north; from October 1644 the city was besieged (or rather, blockaded) by a Scottish army under David Leslie, who was content to wait until shortage of provisions and despair of relief forced a negotiated surrender. Carlisle's governor was Sir Thomas Glemham, previously at York and the man to whom would also fall the dubious honour of surrendering the King's capital, Oxford.

Isaac Tullie, an observant 17-year-old resident of the city, described the course of the siege in considerable detail. It was a leisurely affair. 'The daily skirmishes were none of them for the defence of the walls, which the enemy never assaulted, but about the fetching in of cattle... and now and then the slighting of a work. More was the pity, that such brave men as the besieged should be confined to such worthless adventures such as these...'. There were lighter moments: on 28 March 1645, 'the pleasantness of the day invited Sir Thomas Glemham, with many other Gent. and Gentlewomen, to take the air near Bocherby; against whom the enemy drawing out all their horse, stood to see them course a haire and take it, under their noses'.

Tullie also noted that towards the end 'an order was published to every citizen to bring in their plate to be coyned, which they did chearfully', though they were not thereby exempted from sudden searches for money or plate on their premises. On 30 May 1645 'three shillings pieces were coined out of the cyttysens plate'. A note dated 13 May 1645 gives details of 1,162 oz taken from the city and from 41 citizens, Tullie's mother's contribution being five spoons weighing 6¼ oz. Of this, after loss in melting and working, 1,076 oz were coined at six shillings per ounce into £323, a gain of over £54 of coined specie when set against the normal value of five shillings. Two denominations, shillings and three-shillings, were produced, with similar designs (**8.1**, **8.11**). Not all plate was melted: a shilling in the Hunterian collection, University of Glasgow, appears to have been coined directly from a piece of decorated plate, gilt on one side.

Fig. 8.1 Carlisle besieged, shilling, May 1645. The letters OBS are short for the Latin *obsessum*, 'besieged', or perhaps '*obsidio*', 'siege'. (cf. also 8.5)

According to Tullie's narrative, the City contributed £60 per month towards the soldiers' pay, which came to an end on 24 March 1645; the siege coinage set in train about a month later was presumably a response to this. The news of Naseby (fought 14 June) finally killed all hopes of relief and the city all but ran out of food. The last barrel of strong ale was, however, put to good use. On 23 June, a Scottish commander came into the city to negotiate its surrender, but returned to Leslie so drunk that he could give him 'no account of his errand, nor utter a wise word'. Next day, a 'graver person' was sent in, but fared no better, returning in the same pickle ..., professing that the garrison was everywhere full of strong drink'. The city surrendered the following day.

Scarborough mint

Scarborough was held for the King by Sir Hugh Chomley, previously a parliamentarian. After Marston Moor and the loss of York, he obtained a twenty-day truce in which to negotiate the town's surrender, sending 19 propositions to the Committee of Both Kingdoms in London whose reply, dated 26 August 1644, rejected several. Chomley used the truce to good effect, fortifying the town and gathering in the harvest and other provisions. He was well prepared for a protracted siege.

By February 1645, Chomley was forced to abandon the town, but the castle hung on (**8.2**); Sir John Meldrum made strenuous attempts, which eventually cost him his life, to storm the castle. The garrison held out in increasingly desperate straits until surrendering on terms on 22 July. It is thanks to Chomley's memoir of the siege, prepared in 1647 or 1648 for Sir Edward Hyde (later Earl of Clarendon) for his *History of the Rebellion*, that we have a description of the genesis of siege money:

> The soldiers ... had not only 12 pence a week besides diet, but sixpence for every day's labour, which together with a continual supply to the officers even for necessary accomodations ... had consumed a good sum of monies ...

a

b

Fig. 8.2 a. Scarborough Castle, showing its dominant position on a headland overlooking the town; b. The inner bailey and Henry II's 'great tower' or keep, built 1159-69 and destroyed in the 1645 siege. *E. Besly*

Apart from expecting free billeting of the soldiers,

> The governor bore the greatest part of it upon his own charge and purse, and at last when he wanted money, and could not borrow, having likewise sold the small quantity of plate he had there to defray the public charge, he made a motion that every one that had any plate in the garrison might contribute some part of it to the relief of the soldiers

Not everyone was keen, so Chomley appears to have called in a few favours:

> … but those who had more than double to what was in the garrison besides, were not onlie unwilling to part with any themselves, but underhand wrought upon others to be adverse to itt; so that rather than to breed the least disquiett by taking any man's goods against his will, the Governor made use of the plaite which belonged to some persons hee had particular interest in, which was cutt in pieces, and passed current according to there [*their*] several weights, some of them had the stampe of a broaken castle with this inscription, 'Caroli fortuna resurgam'; by this means the officers and soldiers, which began to be very clamorous, were for the present verie well settled…

Chomley's description of the coins is borne out beautifully by surviving specimens. Two interlocking series may be attributed to Scarborough, with a collective range of at least twenty different denominations, from 4d up to 5s 8d, characterised by the remarkably close adherence of each specimen to the theoretical weight that it represents (**8.3**, **8.4**). All are very rare and the series is bedevilled by later forgeries. On one series we may clearly see a 'broaken' castle (**8.3**); no genuine example bears the 'Caroli fortuna…' legend, though Chomley's reference to this motto is clearly contemporary. There do exist specimens which appear to match Chomley's description (e.g., **8.5**); many are circular, with the motto engraved (usually) around the

Fig. 8.3 Scarborough besieged, one shilling and sixpence (1645), bearing the 'stampe of a broaken castle'. *Courtesy of the Trustees of the British Museum*

castle; the castle of these pieces is not that of the accepted Scarborough siege coins, nor do they bear marks of value. Some of these will be near-contemporary souvenirs of the siege; others may have been made for collectors in the 18th century. At least as early as 1755, they were attributed to the Colchester siege in 1648 (see below).

Fig. 8.4 Scarborough besieged, one shilling and fourpence. This second type, which dovetails neatly into the range of values of Scarborough siege coins, was at one time attributed to Beeston Castle. *Courtesy of the Trustees of the British Museum*

Fig. 8.5 '*Caroli fortuna resurgam*' ('I, the fortune of Charles, shall rise again'): variously attributed to Scarborough and Colchester in the past, it now seems to be certain that some date from the siege. They may have been made as keepsakes (note the lack of a mark of value). The lettering on this example suggests a seventeenth-century date. Courtesy of the *Trustees of the British Museum*

Newark mint

Newark was a royalist fortress from around Christmas 1642, when the Earl of Newcastle placed a garrison there. Controlling an important crossing of the river Trent, Newark was a vital link in royalist communications, enabling them to keep open a supply route between Oxford and the north, posed a strategic threat to the parliamentarian heartlands of eastern England and acted as a base for local raiding. Three attempts were made to take the town: an attempted storming in February 1643; the siege from 29 February to 21 March 1644, Prince Rupert's brilliant relief of which resulted in the capture of Meldrum's entire besieging army; and the final siege from November 1645 to 8 May 1646, when the garrison surrendered by order of the King, who had just given himself up to the Scottish army at Southwell, not far away.

Coins were produced in Newark during this final siege. They are of a single basic design, struck on lozenge-shaped blanks in four denominations (half crown, shilling, ninepence, sixpence) and dated 1645 or 1646 (**8.6**, **8.7**, **8.11**). Their engraving is competent and weights correspond with contemporary official coinage standards. Many of the smaller coins were made directly from cut-up plate, sometimes decorated (**8.6**). One series dated 1646 was produced from gilt plate. Some of these coins have reeded edges and marks where areas of gilding have worn off through use before coining; others bear a royal coat of arms, even the occasional hallmark, overstruck by Newark designs. A royal service of gilt plate of early Stuart date seems to have been sacrificed during the last weeks of the siege.

There are two contemporary references to the Newark siege coinage, both pictorial. A 1645 ninepence is depicted on a plan of the siege (**8.7**), surveyed by Richard Clampe, a parliamentarian engineer who was an eyewitness and perhaps even responsible for laying out the besiegers' lines, as well as recording them. The plan was engraved by Peregrine Lovell (for whom no work later than 1647 is known) and printed and sold by Peter Stent of London, almost certainly before 1650.

Fig. 8.6 Newark besieged, shilling 1645. Cut directly from plate and still showing traces of the grained decoration of the original piece.

The coins themselves have survived in considerable numbers and seem to have been prized as souvenirs – many have been pierced for suspension or for attachment to clothing. When Anthony Ascham, Commonwealth ambassador to Spain, was murdered in Madrid in June 1650, a Newark shilling, perhaps retooled as an amulet if the drawing that was published is to be believed, was found on his body 'on his left side next his skinne'. Their currency, however, was strictly local and modern finds of siege money are very few. Two 1646 Newark ninepences were found in 1960 with other coins accompanying a skeleton buried on the outskirts of Newark itself; another ninepence, dated 1645 and pierced as a keepsake, came to light in 2006 at Mareham le Fen, Lincolnshire, about 25 miles away.

The designs of the Carlisle and Newark siege issues are in effect identical: the one presumably inspired the other. But what inspired the first? Many Civil War commanders saw service in Europe during the Thirty Years' War and may well have been familiar with the Low Countries sieges and coins using the formula 'OBS'; Sir Thomas Glemham is known to have served in the German wars, where John Bellasis, Governor of Newark, was probably too young to have done so. There is, however, no obvious single design source. If one is to be sought, perhaps we should look to Ireland and the 'crowned C R' issues of the Lords Justices in Dublin in 1643 (below, p.123).

Fig. 8.7 Richard Clampe's plan of the siege of Newark, 1646, showing royalist and parliamentarian fortifications and a Newark siege coin. (Size of original 20 x 17 inches/509 x 432 mm). *British Library, Maps *4670.(1)*

The 'Second Civil War': Pontefract

After the King's surrender in May 1646, there followed two years of uneasy peace, but in the spring of 1648 there was a series of risings by royalists and disaffected former parliamentarians in several parts of England and Wales, which has come to be known as the 'Second Civil War'. Mostly, these were quickly suppressed. From Pembrokeshire, an army led by Major General Rowland Laugharne (as a Parliament man the successful besieger of Aberystwyth Castle in 1646) drove all before it until defeated at St Fagans, near Cardiff, on 8 May; Cromwell himself supervised the final reduction of Pembroke Castle. An army formed in Kent was driven into Essex and took refuge in Colchester, which fell to Fairfax only after a bitter siege lasting from 13 June to 28 August. Eventually shortage of food and ammunition forced the garrison to surrender; the royalist commanders rendered themselves 'to mercy', which for Sir George Lisle and Sir Charles Lucas meant summary execution.

The Yorkshire castle of Pontefract, the 'key to the north' (**8.8**), was seized for the King in a bloodless coup by Colonel John Morris on 2 June 1648, but the defeat of the invading Scottish army by Cromwell at Preston (17 August) left it isolated and from October the castle underwent its third siege of the war years. The siege was at first desultory, but the arrival of General Rainsborough and his subsequent killing at Doncaster in a daring royalist commando raid led to a more vigorous and close siege by General Lambert. Even so, the garrison held out until 22 March 1649, nearly two months after Charles I's death. Their leaders, as at Colchester, were exempted from mercy, but most contrived to escape. Morris and a companion were eventually captured and killed. By 5 April 1649, the castle had been demolished, at a cost of £1,779 17s 4d, which was all recouped by selling the materials, notably lead, which alone raised over £1,500.

Two series of coins, mainly shillings, but including gold twenty-shillings, were struck by the defenders, before (**8.9a**) and after (**8.10**) the King's death, the second series being the first coins to be struck in the name of Charles II. A Pontefract coin, probably of the type of **8.9**, is mentioned in a contemporary newspaper, *The Kingdom's Faithful and Impartial Scout*:

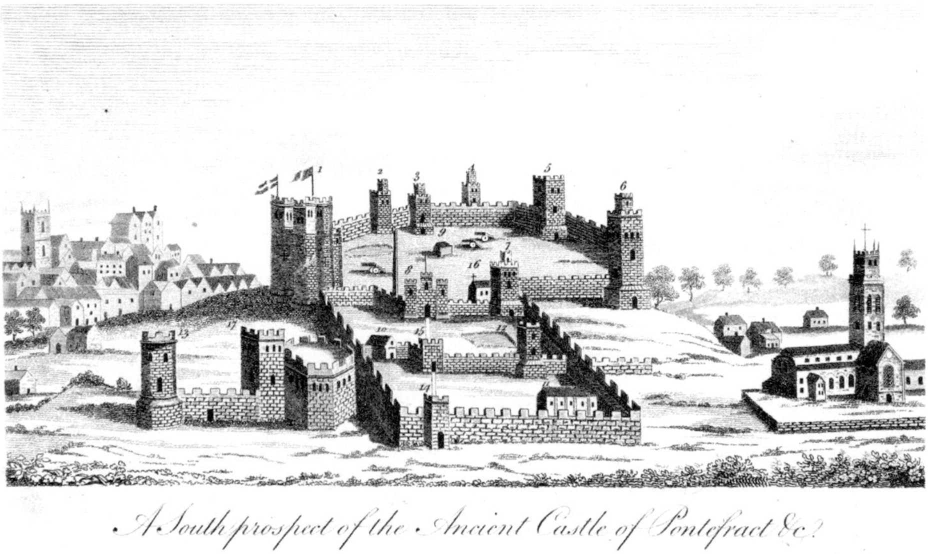

Fig. 8.8 A view of Pontefract Castle, from G. Fox, *the History of Pontefract*, 1827. *National Museum of Wales Library*.

> [Monday, February 5th] … The besieged have lately made two sallies forth but repulsed without any great losse to us; in the last … we took two of theirs prisoners, one of which had a small parcel of silver in his pocket, somewhat square; on the one side thereof was stamped a castle with PO for Pontefract, and the other was a crown with CR on each side of it. These pieces they make of plate, which they get out of the country, and pass among them for coyn.

Excavations at Pontefract Castle have produced evidence of the defenders' minting activities in the form of lead trial pieces for some of the issues (**8.9b**). Several siege coins are said to have been found in local gardens, but details are now lost.

a.

b.

Fig. 8.9 a: Pontefact besieged, lozenge-shaped shilling, 1648. Note the flaw on the C of P – C (which thus resembles an O) and the possible remains of a date letter or other hallmark at the top of the obverse. b: Lead trial piece for the same issue, excavated at Pontefract Castle. (b): *Courtesy of Wakefield Council*.

Fig. 8.10 Pontefract besieged, shillings in the name of Charles II, '1648' [OS], the first coupled with a 'lifetime' reverse of Charles I; the second bears the (Latin) legend 'for the son, after the father's death'.

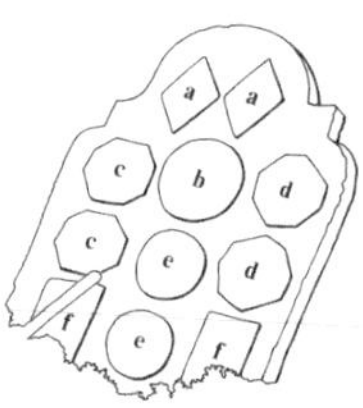

Fig. 8.11 'Siege Coins': an engraving from *Coins, Medals, Ancient Buildings and other Antiquities relative to the English History*, published by R. Bowyer, 1794. The coins, which are faithfully depicted, are: a. Newark half crown, 1646; b. '*Caroli fortuna resurgam*'; c. Pontefract shilling, struck before the King's death; d. Pontefract shilling of Charles II; e. Carlisle three shillings, 1645; f. Scarborough half crown(?), with later engraving on the reverse. The engraver, John Landseer, was the father of the celebrated Victorian Academician, Sir Edwin. *Courtesy of the Trustees of the British Museum*

Fig. 8.12 Gold 'ten shillings' piece bearing the date 1648; perhaps a relic of the siege of Colchester. *Courtesy of the Trustees of the British Museum*

Colchester siege pieces?

Two sorts of 'siege piece' have been attributed to the Colchester siege of June-August 1648: a gold bracteate 'ten shillings', now in the British Museum (**8.12**), which may be a relic of the siege and *Caroli fortuna resurgam* pieces, which certainly are not. The gold piece bears in a single design all of the conventional elements of an emergency coinage and appears to have been fashioned, using a die or matrix, from some other worked object; the 'castle' on it is a curious blend of fortress and country house. We cannot be sure of this object's date, other than that it can be traced at least to the Tyssen sale in April-May 1802.

Unlike the other siege coinages discussed in this chapter, there is no contemporary reference to any siege issue at Colchester. There is no definitive answer to the question, but attribution of coinage to Colchester appears to be an eighteenth-century idea. The siege itself was qualitatively different from the others for which coinages have been reported: it was relatively short, close and fierce and unlike in 1645-6 there was little opportunity for soldiers to slip away, give themselves up or change sides – little likelihood this time of a quiet pardon and return home. Commitment was unquestioned and did not have to be bought. In other words, conditions did not exist for a siege coinage to be needed.

Chapter 9

IRELAND

Events in Ireland left their mark on the contemporary coinage. The revolt of October 1641 led to the establishment of an insurgent Catholic government in Kilkenny, while English control was restricted to the area around Dublin and an enclave in Munster centred on present day County Cork. The need to suppress the rebellion brought to a head the tensions between King and Parliament over control of the armed forces in the months leading to civil war in England itself.

Both sides in the Irish conflict minted 'coinages of necessity'. The Confederated Catholics produced copper small change, proclaimed, along with revaluations of other current coinage, on 15 November 1642. Two issues of silver have also been attributed to them. The first was ordered to be coined from plate with the 'ordinary stamp used in the moneyes now currant' and has been identified with the crude half crowns known as Blacksmith's Money (**9.1**). These copy Tower half crowns from the early part of the reign, i.e. 'money now currant' in that since 1637 payments in English money had been obligatory in Ireland, replacing the various 'Irish' and foreign types that had hitherto circulated. A second explanation of the type ascribes it to Kilkenny, as an issue of the royalists in 1649 (see below). However, the finding in the Tregwynt hoard in 1996 of an example of the Blacksmith's

Fig. 9.1 Half crown, 'Blacksmith's Money', privy-marks Cross and Harp. Probably produced by the Confederated Catholics in 1642. *Tregwynt Treasure Trove*

half crown would appear to strengthen the Confederated Catholics theory, for the hoard was most likely buried by the spring of 1648 and the coin does appear to be a bit worn. Their second likely issue, known as 'Rebel Money' was produced during 1643 and comprised crowns and half crowns bearing as designs a large cross and their respective values (**9.2**).

Fig. 9.2 'Rebel Money', silver crown of reduced weight (24.43g), traditionally ascribed to the Confederated Catholics. It has also been suggested that this coinage may have been issued by officials at Dublin Castle under Col. Michael Jones, Deputy Governor under the English Parliament *c*.1648.

The Lords, Justices and Council of Ireland appealed repeatedly for both troops and money from England to suppress the rebellion. In January 1643 they collected plate in Dublin (about £1,200 worth) which was turned into silver coinage stamped with the weights of each denomination ('Inchiquin money', **9.3**); on some of the smallest the value in pence was also indicated by a number of small rings, the so-called 'annulets' issue. A second group of crowns and half crowns was simply stamped with the appropriate value ('Dublin Money', **9.4**). These coins were all produced to Tower standards of weight and fineness. A half crown of the first issue was found near Urchfont, Wiltshire in 2011.

A further coinage, for which royal approval was sought and received, was proclaimed in Dublin on 8 July 1643. Its designs were specified by the King in a letter written from Oxford on 25 May, and the standards again matched the English. The Lords Justices were authorized to melt down plate, etc., into

Fig. 9.3 Half crown of the Lords Justices' first issue, 1643. The design is the same on both sides and the declared weight (9dwt and 16 grains, or 15.03 grammes) matches that of an English half crown.

Fig. 9.4 'Dublin Money': a half crown similar to 9.3, but stamped on both sides with its value. *Spink & Son Ltd*

> Small peeces, to the value of five shillings, halfe-crowns, twelve pences, six-pences, or of any less value, which severall small peeces they shall make the same weight, value and allay, as our moneys now currant in England of those values respectively are, and shall stamp the same on the one side, with these letters (scilicet) C.R. for Carolus Rex, with a crown over those letters, and on the other side with the values of the said severall peeces respectively.

The new coinage was produced by Sir John Veale and two prominent Dublin goldsmiths, Peter Vaneyndhoven and Gilbert Tonges, who entered into a recognizance of £2,000 for the true making of the coins, which were to be delivered to the bringers of the plate – in the normal fashion, that is. An eighth part was required to be coined as groats, threepences and twopences. On 13 October 1643, the issue was declared legal tender in England, no doubt with an eye to the forces recently freed by the truce ('cessation') on 15 September to leave for England to fight for the King. These coins do indeed occasionally turn up on the 'mainland': in Wales, a groat from Wisemans Bridge, Pembrokeshire and a crown in the Tregwynt hoard (**9.5**), the only example from a securely Civil-War context; a threepence of the issue was found at Aldford, Cheshire in 2007. This coinage is commonly known as 'Ormonde money' – James Butler, 12th Earl and subsequently first Duke of Ormonde, Lieutenant-General of the King's forces in Ireland and later Lord-Lieutenant, was a signatory of the July proclamation (**9.6**). Its distinctive design may have served as a model for some of the English siege coinages (see above, p.113).

Fig. 9.5 Crown of the Lords Justices' issue of 1643-4, called 'Ormonde Money'. *Tregwynt Treasure Trove*

Ormonde was responsible for two further issues of coinage in Ireland. On 29 July 1646 he authorized Vaneyndhoven and Tonges to produce gold 'pledges' from bullion to hand, to be marked with their weights (4 pennyweight 7 grains and 8 dwt 14 gr), equivalent to Spanish pistoles and double pistoles current in Ireland, though at a lower fineness of 19 carats (79%). On 1 February 1647 civilians were encouraged to submit bullion for similar coining, but at a higher fineness ('betwixt 20 and 22 carrotts':

83.3 – 91.6%), corresponding to that of the Spanish coins. Ormonde's gold (**9.7**) is extremely rare today – only two double pistoles, which come to us from the collection of the Earls of Bridgewater, and eleven pistoles are known, six of these from a single hoard found in 1946-8 at Derryville, Portarlington, Co. Laois.

Fig. 9.6 James Butler, 12th Earl (afterwards 1st Duke) of Ormonde; attributed to Justus van Egmont (1601-74). *Courtesy of the Claydon House Trust*

In July 1647 Ormonde left Ireland, having handed Dublin over to a parliamentary expedition. However, he returned in September 1648 to lead a united royalist alliance. Silver crowns and half crowns similar to those of the second 1643 issue, but bearing the name and titles of Charles II were probably issued by him in 1649 (**9.8**); their place of minting is uncertain (it cannot be Dublin). It is tempting to associate this issue with Ormonde's warrant of 8 August 1649 for establishing a mint at Kilkenny (which remained in royalist hands until 28 March 1650), but this specified 'the coyning of gould and silver according to the way manner and form formerly used in England…' and it is uncertain whether Ormonde's Kilkenny mint ever functioned.

Fig. 9.7 Gold pistole of Ormonde's 1646 or 1647 issue. *Spink & Son Ltd*

Fig. 9.8 Half crown in the name of Charles II, issued by Ormonde in 1649.

Some crude copper 'coins' from Bandon, Cork, Kinsale and Youghal (the last dated 1646), long held to be siege or necessity pieces of the southern 'cities of refuge', are now regarded as an early segment of the Irish token series. Bandon, Kinsale and Youghal examples are amongst many Irish tokens found in recent years in traders' ballast dumps at Black Pill,

Swansea Bay in South Wales. The Youghal pieces (**9.9**) were proclaimed at Cork on 20 March 1646, to be current throughout the English enclave as small change, with provisions for their exchange and limits on the amounts qualifying as legal tender, reminiscent of the farthing tokens in England. Silver shillings and sixpences were, however, struck in Cork in 1647.

Fig. 9.9 Token farthing for the English enclave in Munster, Youghal 1646. *Spink & Son Ltd*

Chapter 10

THE TOWER MINT IN THE CIVIL WAR

Parliament seized control of the Mint in the Tower of London on 10 August 1642, though it was not until 5 October that the staff were formally forbidden to leave their posts. The joint Masters, Sir Ralph Freeman and Sir Thomas Aylesbury were ejected; the Warden, Sir William Parkhurst had joined the King, and was to become Charles's joint, later sole Master at the Oxford mint. Aylesbury, too, reappeared at Oxford, though not in the context of the mint (p.45). In the event, few others had joined the King; most mint workers took the simplest course and remained where they were. (Similarly, those moneyers seconded to Bushell at Aberystwyth served the royalists at Shrewsbury, Oxford and Bristol.) There was plenty of work at the Tower: to the continuing massive amounts of Spanish silver were added large quantities of plate contributed more or less voluntarily by the citizens of London and those of Puritan persuasion elsewhere. Modest contributions, such as the 12½ ounces valued at £3 6s 8d, received from Nathan King, chandler, on 28 November 1642, also had their place.

The Parliament, anxious to maintain the fiction that it was fighting on behalf of the King, was reluctant to usurp the royal prerogative of coinage, especially since at first military success was by no means certain. The appearance of the coins therefore remained the same and their dies continued to be made from the same design- and letter-punches. The annual alteration of the privy-mark and the pyx trial were overlooked in the spring of 1642, though an interim account of the bullion melted and coined from 1 April 1641 to 31 March 1642 was drawn up. The existing mark, a triangle within a circle, continued in use for a further year. The coins bearing this mark therefore tend to dominate in many Civil War hoards, not only because so many were struck (about £2 million in silver alone), but also because this was the last Tower issue to pass into circulation throughout the country before communications became difficult (**10.1**). A new Master was not appointed until 6 May 1643, when Sir Robert Harley returned to the post he had previously held from 1626 until 1635. At the same time, a new privy-mark, 'P-in-brackets' (**10.2**) hinted that control of the Mint now lay with Parliament and the 'Triangle-in-circle' coins were finally pyxed.

Fig. 10.1 Tower half crown, privy-mark Triangle-in-circle, 1641-3. *Penybryn Treasure Trove*

Fig. 10.2 Tower gold twenty shillings, p.m. *P-in-brackets*, under parliamentary control, 1643-4.

Output continued at a high level during the war years, fuelled mainly by the Spanish silver (about £1 million each year, 95% of it in silver). Weight and fineness were maintained, but many coins were poorly produced. The Mint had taken delivery of five iron presses of unspecified type in 1640 and a further eleven in 1642, but it was not a good time for experiment. There is no hint from the products that these were ever used; the coins show every sign of having been made by traditional manual methods, at great speed (**10.3**).

Fig. 10.3 Tower shilling, p.m. *R-in-brackets*, under Parliament, 1644-5. Despite its appearance, this is an unworn coin of full weight, but poorly produced. *Penybryn Treasure Trove*

Table V: *The Tower Mint: Privy-marks and pyx trials under Parliament, 1643-9*

	Triangle-in-circle	29 May 1643
(P)	P-in-brackets	15 July 1644
(R)	R-in-brackets	12 May 1645
	Eye	10 November 1645
	Sun	15 February 1647
	Sceptre	9 November 1649

The areas controlled by Parliament always formed a more coherent whole than those of the royalists, with control of the capital, all routes leading from it and most of the south and east coasts. No branch mints were opened, though serious consideration was given to the idea of a mint at Exeter early in the war. This was discussed in the Commons on 8 December 1642 and on 3 January 1643 a mint and moneyers were ordered to be dispatched to Exeter. At some point one William Gobell of the Mint did indeed go to Exeter, but plate gathered during the royalist siege was never coined, for reasons that are not entirely clear. It formed one of the bones of contention the following year in a dispute between Philip Francis, a former mayor of Plymouth, and Charles Vaughan, Parliamentary Treasurer of Devon. During the siege, the Exeter goldsmiths Edward Anthony and William Bartlett, as treasurers of the Parliamentarian defence fund, received nearly £4,500 in money and plate, about half of which may have been plate. In 1644, Vaughan admitted that £1,300-worth of plate had been brought in, but claimed that it had been sent to London to buy arms. In any case, Exeter fell to the royalists in September 1643, after a siege of two and a half months; the Parliamentary mint was still-born, but the royalists soon set up their own in the city (Chapter 4, above).

Nevertheless, the increasing scale of the war effort brought problems of cash flow for Parliament, just as for its opponents. On 22 July 1643 an Ordinance was passed for the 'Speedy Raising and Levying of Monies, set by way of a charge or new Impost on … commodities', such as tobacco, wine, beer and various imported groceries and goods, otherwise known as the Excise. It was promptly imitated by the royalists and despite both sides' protestations that it would be 'laide down and utterly abolished' at the end of the war, it proved too useful to abandon and remains with us today. In 1644 Parliament found it necessary to limit immediate costs by paying only a proportion of the sums owing in soldiers' pay, and issuing certificates promising repayment, or personal debentures.

The case of the army of the Eastern Association gives us some idea of the costs involved. Its monthly pay, based on a muster in September 1644, has been estimated at around £31,000, though in the event the cavalry each received only 126 days' pay in 1644 and the infantry around 250 (and this army was better paid than some). Similarly, a subsidy of £30,000 per month was promised as the price of the Scots entering England on Parliament's side, but special efforts to raise this sum (**10.4**) failed to ensure that they were paid in full when they finally arrived in 1644; the inhabitants of northern England suffered accordingly. It is little wonder that the smaller, distant, but important armies of the Fairfaxes in Yorkshire and Sir William

Brereton in Cheshire were forever waiting for their pay. On 18 June 1644 Ferdinando Lord Fairfax (father of Sir Thomas), who estimated that his army pay came to £15,000 per month, wrote to London from his quarters outside York that he had only received £10,000 in the past four months.

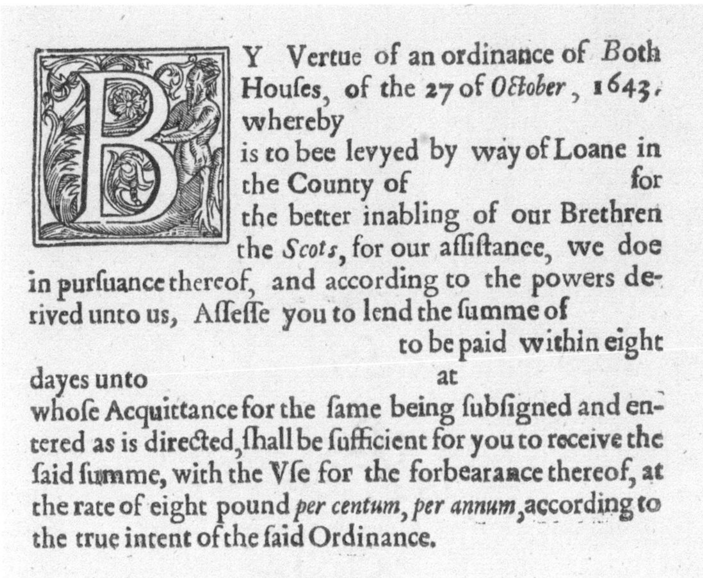

BY Vertue of an ordinance of Both Houſes, of the 27 of *October*, 1643, whereby is to bee levyed by way of Loane in the County of for the better inabling of our Brethren the *Scots*, for our aſſiſtance, we doe in purſuance thereof, and according to the powers derived unto us, Aſſeſſe you to lend the ſumme of to be paid within eight dayes unto at whoſe Acquittance for the ſame being ſubſigned and entered as is directed, ſhall be ſufficient for you to receive the ſaid ſumme, with the Vſe for the forbearance thereof, at the rate of eight pound *per centum*, *per annum*, according to the true intent of the ſaid Ordinance.

Fig. 10.4 Parliamentary assessment for the levy to pay the Scottish army, October 1643. Another forced loan, bearing notional interest at the standard 8%. *British Library C112.h4 (98)*

It seems to be the case that there was simply not enough money available in circulation to meet all of the demands placed upon it. It is clear that from the outset of the war, large amounts of money were withdrawn from circulation, by hoarding, and the compositions of successive hoards through these years testify to the distortion of the circulating medium caused by this. Although the Mint continued to issue huge amounts of silver coinage, much of this new money may equally have gone to ground, in the Parliamentary heartlands. A large hoard found at Ashdon, Essex, in 1984 contained considerable numbers of mint-fresh Tower coins of the years 1643-5; it may exemplify the profits to be made from supplying goods and services to the Parliamentary war effort.

Like their royalist counterparts, the parliamentarians produced medals to commemorate events and as military rewards. The Earl of Essex, Sir William Waller, the Earl of Manchester, Ferdinando Lord Fairfax and his son Sir Thomas (**10.5**) were among commanders depicted, for the most part, on oval badges. Several are the work of Thomas Simon, who with Edward Wade was appointed joint chief engraver on 4 April 1645, following the death of Edward Green (chief engraver, 1626-45). Simon, whose work was to dominate the coins and medals of the Commonwealth and Protectorate, was apprenticed to Green on 25 September 1635 and also learnt much from the work of Briot. The 'Scots Rebellion' medals of 1639 are early works of his (**4.15**). By the time his apprenticeship ended, war was breaking out. He remained loyal to Parliament and in 1643 committed what royalists regarded as high treason by engraving a duplicate Great Seal for Parliament's use after the original had been taken to the King at York.

In spite of his surrender in 1646 and subsequent captivity, Charles remained King and the coinage continued to be struck in his name. New portrait punches were prepared and although there may appear to be an element of caricature in some of these, the equestrian effigy which was introduced in 1646 is a fine creation (**10.6**). It is normally attributed to Thomas Simon and is very similar to his design approved for half crowns of Charles II's first coinage in 1660, which was not in the event used. Output from the

Fig. 10.6 Tower crown, p.m. Sun, 1645-7, with new equestrian portrait attributed to Thomas Simon. *Courtesy of the Trustees of the British Museum*

Fig. 10.5 Sir Thomas Fairfax, gold military reward by Thomas Simon, 1645; probably given to officers who had served under Fairfax at Marston Moor, this one to John Sharpe. Perhaps the greatest of the Parliament's generals, Fairfax was also scrupulously fair to defeated royalists (notably, in our context, Sir Richard Vyvyan). When Oxford surrendered, Fairfax's first act was to 'sett a good guard of soldiers to preserve the Bodleian Library' (Aubrey). On occasion, he could be ruthless, as in the execution of Lucas and Lisle at Colchester in 1648. *Courtesy of the Trustees of the British Museum*

Tower dropped dramatically in 1647 as the Thirty Years War drew towards its end and the Spanish found it cheaper to use Dutch carriers to transport their silver. The coins of Charles's last years are therefore relatively scarce.

Aberystwyth revived

With conditions relatively settled and new silver once again scarce, the revival of the Welsh branch mint became an attractive proposition. On 6 March 1647 Edmund Goodere, Bushell's partner in the Cardiganshire mines, petitioned the House of Lords for permission to reopen the Aberystwyth mint, but at 'a place called the smelting mills, near the refining house', on account of the siege-damage to the castle at Aberystwyth, where the pre-war mint had been situated (p.20). The premises, between Talybont and Machynlleth, subsequently became the iron-smelting Dyfi Furnace, where excavations have shown that few traces now remain of the seventeenth-century 'silver mills' phase (**10.7**). As before, the Tower Mint provided dies and workmen. The date of the re-opening is not known, but the small output may have been made late in 1648. The King's execution on 30 January 1649 was soon followed by closure of the mint; its dies and equipment were surrendered to a parliamentary representative on 23 February.

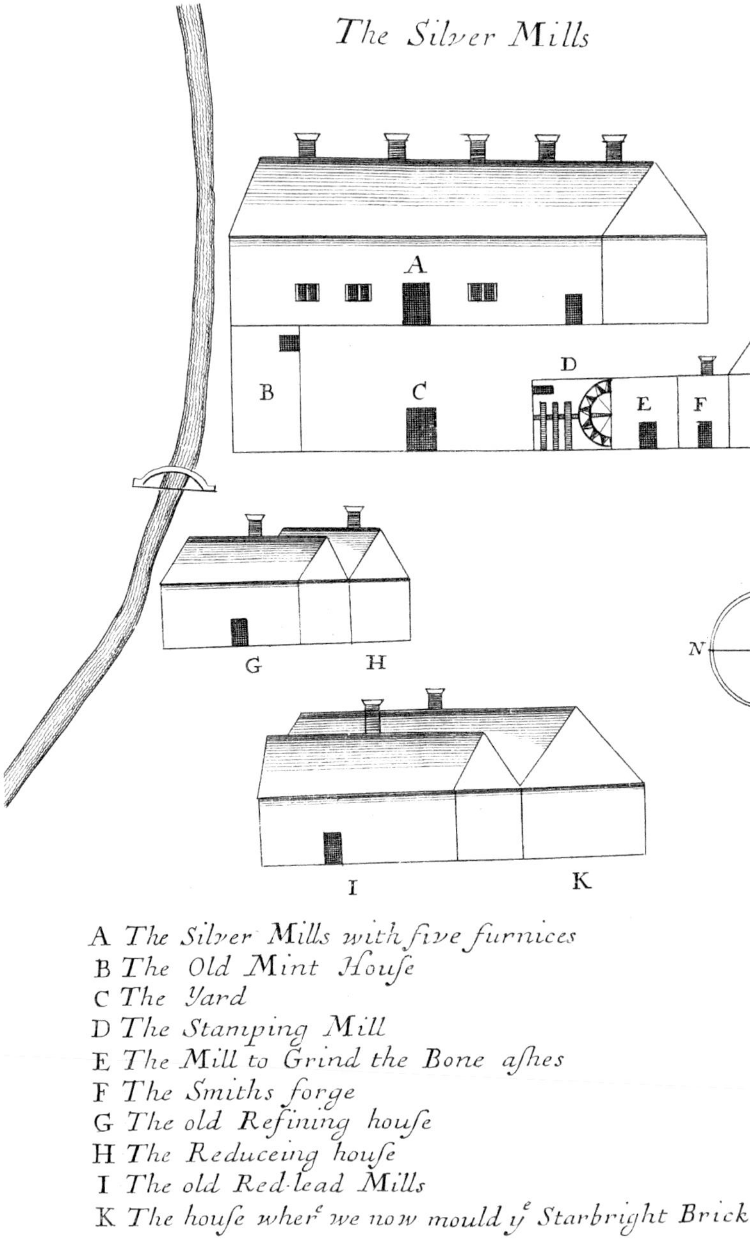

Fig. 10.7 The Silver Mills, Talybont, Cardiganshire, showing the Old Mint House (at B). From W. Waller, *An Account of the Cardiganshire Mines*, London, n.d. [1704]. *National Museum of Wales Library.*

The coins struck at the Silver Mills are similar in design to pre-war Aberystwyth products, but with a crown as privy-mark (**10.8**). The same denominations were made, excepting only halfpence. These types were for a long time assigned to a mythical mint at Combe Martin in Devon, where Bushell attempted to revive flooded silver mines in 1648, but the 'Welsh' designs and the close correspondence of surviving coins to the list of dies surrendered at the Silver Mills suggest that the 'crown' coins are indeed products of the briefly-restored Aberystwyth operation. Isotopic analysis of lead traces confirmed that these coins are of silver from the same source as was used for the pre-war Aberystwyth issues.

Fig. 10.8 Half crown, sixpence, threepence and half groat, struck at the Silver Mills, 1648-9, all with p.m. *Crown* and the Welsh feathers. (For a Tower Mint half crown with p.m. *Crown*, see 1.9: these and the prolific *Crown*-marked shillings are often mistakenly thought to be Silver Mills products.)

Chapter 11

AFTERMATH

The story of the Civil War and its coinage does not end with the death of Charles I. As we have seen the siege of Pontefract was maintained, and military action in Scotland and Ireland continued until 1652. Britain was to remain a republic for a further eight years before Charles II returned in 1660, in what he termed the twelfth year of his reign. This last chapter therefore describes some of the coins and medals of the final phase of the Great Rebellion and its aftermath.

The Commonwealth and Protectorate, 1649-60

The Kingly office was abolished by Act of Parliament on 17 March 1649 and Thomas Simon was commissioned to cut a new Great Seal for the 'Commonwealth of England'. Meanwhile, moves were under way to establish a new coinage, the Act for which was finally passed on 17 July. In May, Sir Robert Harley was dismissed as Master for refusing to have anything to do with the new coinage and Dr Aaron Guerdain was appointed in his stead. (A pyx trial of Charles I's last ('*Sceptre*') coinage, at Harley's expense, was ordered on 16 May 1949, but not held until 9 November.) In a radical departure from previous practice, the legends of the new money were in English and common designs were chosen for all denominations from the gold twenty shillings down to the silver penny (**11.1**), with a simplified version for the tiny halfpenny. These became a standing joke amongst royalist sympathisers, who described the conjoined shields of the reverse as 'breeches for the Rump' (a reference to the depleted membership of the Long Parliament) and observed from the legends 'The Commonwealth of England' and 'God with us', that God and the Commonwealth were on different sides.

Fig. 11.1 Commonwealth of England: gold double crown (10 shillings), 1649; silver half crown, 1649; half groat, undated. All of uniform design, struck at the Tower of London.

In 1650, Cromwell's brutal subjugation of the Irish was interrupted when he had to return to the mainland to lead the campaign against the Scots. Despite his being trapped at Dunbar he routed the Scots on 3 September and on the 7th the Commons resolved that special thanks be conveyed to the Lord General, also to the officers and soldiers of the army 'and that a number of gold and silver medals be distributed amongst them'. Thomas Simon was ordered to Scotland to take Cromwell's likeness for the medal. The sitter expressed his own ideas for its design in a letter to the Committee of the Army, 4 February 1651:

> It was not a little wonder to me to see that you should send Mr Symonds so great a journey about a business importinge so little as farr as it relates to me, when as if my poor opinion may not be rejected by you, I have to offer to that which I thinke the most noble

> end, to witt the commemoration of the great mercie att Dunbar, & the gratuitie to the army which might be better expressed upon the medall by engraving on the one side the Parliament which I heare was intended & will do singularly well, so on the other side an army with this inscription over the head of it, The Lord of hosts, which was our word that day, whereof if I may beg it as a favour from you I most earnestly beseech you if I may doe it without offence that it may be soe, & if you think not fit to have it as I offer, you may alter it as you see Cause only I doe think I may truly say it wilbe verie thankfully acknowledged by me, if you will spare the having my effigies on it.

The Dunbar Medal (**11.2**) was the first British award intended to be given to officers and men alike for a particular action, but it remains doubtful that a general distribution ever took place; once later restrikes and forgeries are eliminated, very few original specimens appear to survive today. The Commonwealth years also saw the beginning of systematic rewarding of meritorious service at sea, a topic that has been systematically studied by Marvin Lessen. The recent work of J.J. and A.K. Platt provides a comprehensive coverage of the medallic record of the entire period of the 'Civil Wars' (see Further Reading).

Fig. 11.2 The small 'Dunbar Medal', in gold, by Thomas Simon. Cromwell's request not to appear on the medal was clearly ignored, though an army and the parliamentary watchword were included. *Courtesy of the Trustees of the British Museum*

The final mainland battle of the Civil War was not fought until 3 September 1651, when Charles II and his Scottish army were defeated at Worcester, again by Cromwell, the 'crowning mercy'.

Attention once again turned to the mechanization of coin production and the marking of their edges, to deter counterfeiting and clipping. Another Frenchman, Pierre Blondeau, was summoned to London, arriving in September 1649; but at first he could not proceed, because of opposition from the moneyers. Trials were made in 1651, both by Blondeau (**11.3**) and David Ramage, Briot's former pupil, representing the moneyers. In 1656, Blondeau was ordered to produce a small issue of coins bearing Cromwell's portrait, using dies made by Thomas Simon, newly created chief engraver of the Mint. The project was revived in 1658, but cut short by Cromwell's death and Blondeau returned to France. The Cromwell coins do not seem to have been issued for circulation, and are not mentioned in the 1661 proclamation which called in the issues of the Commonwealth. Indeed, these regal-looking coins (**11.4**; compare with **11.5**, a warts-and-all portrait) soon commanded a premium as collectors' pieces after the Restoration of Charles II, the diarist Samuel Pepys noting on 9 March 1662 that the silver crowns 'are now sold it seems for 25s and 30s a-piece'. Further examples were made subsequently using new dies cut from Simon's punches, both in London and the Low Countries.

Fig. 11.3 Pattern shilling by Blondeau, London 1651. Blondeau's design matches that of the Commonwealth coinage; Ramage varied the designs and omitted the values.

Provision of the smallest change remained inadequate and the Interregnum saw the beginnings of a rash of token-issues by town corporations and individual traders, which reached its peak in the first years of Charles II's reign (**11.6** and see *Further Reading*). Adequate supplies of official copper farthings and halfpence were eventually produced in the 1670s.

Fig. 11.4 Oliver Cromwell, half crown 1658. The edge of the coin bears the words HAS:NISI:PERITVRVS:MIHI:ADIMAT:NEMO (Let no-one remove these from me on pain of death), marked by Blondeau's secret new process.

Fig. 11.5 After Sir Peter Lely (1616-80), *Oliver Cromwell* (1599-1658), 17th century, oil on canvas. *National Museum of Wales, Department of Art (A 5366).*

The Monarchy restored

On 29 May 1660, Charles II returned to England and the new King was showered with petitions for jobs, money or for pardon, from mint-employees no less than others. Former mint officials loyal to his father were restored to their positions and an indenture with the newly-restored Master,

Sir Ralph Freeman, provided for coinage of the same pieces and values as in the time of the late King. Sir William Parkhurst resumed his post of Warden, jointly with Sir Anthony St Leger.

Thomas Simon sought the post of Chief Engraver to his Majesty and the Mint 'which he had held under the late King, and for pardon, because by order of Parliament he made their Great Seal in 1643, and was their Chief graver of the Mint and seals'. However Thomas Rawlins, Charles I's wartime engraver, was restored (at least in name) on 7 July. Simon seems to have done most of the work and a warrant dated 25 August 1660 approving designs for the first coins of Charles II was addressed to him, but he had to be content with the office of one of the engravers of the King's arms, shields and stamps (31 May 1661). He had not helped his cause by his dilatoriness in producing the new puncheons and dies, which drew several sharp reminders; his former treason in producing a duplicate Great Seal in 1643, for the Parliament's use, had not been forgiven. Rawlins, meanwhile, seems to have worked on seals, such as the judicial seals for the Welsh circuits, completed on 24 September 1660. The new coinage finally appeared in February 1661. On the 19th, Samuel Pepys saw some of the dies: 'we met with Mr Slingsby [the Deputy Master], … who showed me the stamps of the King's new coyne; which is strange to see how good they are in the stamp and bad in the money, for lack of skill to make them. But he says that Blondeau will shortly come over and then we shall have it better, and the best in the world'. Change was in the air.

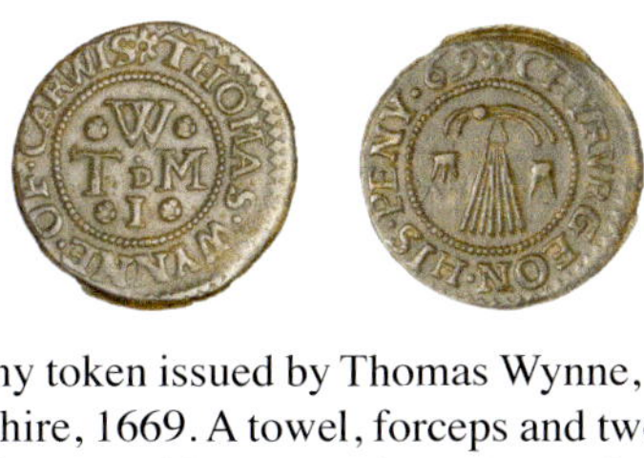

Fig. 11.6 Penny token issued by Thomas Wynne, 'Chyrurgeon' of Caerwys, Flintshire, 1669. A towel, forceps and two extracted teeth bear graphic witness to his occupation. Most tokens of the period were farthings and halfpence, but in some remoter areas, such as North Wales, pennies are relatively common.

Meanwhile, coins of the Commonwealth were allowed to circulate for the time being, alongside the 'lawful money'. On 7 September 1661 it was proclaimed that they would cease to be current from the end of November, after which they were to be brought to the Mint and exchanged for an equal quantity of lawful money. (They were, of course, of the same weight and fineness; counterfeiting them continued to carry the same penalties.) A period of grace was allowed, during which they continued to be accepted in tax payments. After some discussion, 1 March 1662 was made the final deadline for their surrender. The third, and biggest, of Charles II's hammered coinages thus represents the final coinage of the Civil War, as the cross and harp money of the 'late usurpation' went into the melting pot (**11.7**). Recoinage seems to have been thorough, even though only some two-thirds of the estimated output of around £1 million was recovered. Much of the rest had no doubt already gone abroad (sold to foreign mints, or servicing a balance of payments deficit) and some was hoarded. Commonwealth coins, notably the smallest types, are occasionally found today in a worn state, while the odd surviving specimen bears the central perforation relating to the great recoinage of 1696. But they are almost never found in post-Restoration hoards, through conscious exclusion as much as scarcity, perhaps.

The recoinage was also the last issue to be made at the Tower by traditional methods. In 1661 it was decided to abandon manual techniques in favour of machinery, and on 8 November Simon was sent to France to fetch Blondeau to supervise the mechanisation of the Mint, to supply equipment and to train the moneyers in the new methods of coining by mill and press. The famous competition between Thomas Simon and John Roettier, who with his brothers Joseph and Philip was summoned from Flanders by the King, was ordered on 7 February 1662. Each artist was to produce a trial piece of crown size for consideration by the King. Roettier's was preferred, perhaps because Simon, the perfectionist, failed to produce his at all. In all events, the famous Petition Crown by Simon is dated 1663, a good year later than the trial itself (**11.8**).

Fig. 11.7 Charles II, half crown of the 'third hammered issue', 1661-2. A splendid piece which does rare justice to Simon's portraiture. Continuity and legality are underlined by the use of the same motto as his father and a crown as privy-mark; innovation, in the use of a profile portrait on a half crown.

Fig. 11.8 The 'Petition Crown' by Thomas Simon, 1663. Fine work, but perhaps too close to life; Roettier's somewhat idealised portraiture was preferred. The legend placed on the edge is a *tour-de-force* of miniature engraving: **THOMAS SIMON** MOST HVMBLY PRAYS YOVR **MAJESTY** TO COMPARE THIS HIS TRYALL PIECE WITH THE DVTCH AND IF MORE TRVLY DRAWN & EMBOSS'D MORE GRACE FVLLY ORDER'D AND MORE ACCVRATELY ENGRAVEN TO RELEIVE HIM. *Spink & Son Ltd*

From February 1663 all new money made at the Mint was made mechanically. The long thin ingots were subjected to two rolling operations, after which blanks were made by a screw-driven cutter press. These were then weighed and any which were too heavy were filed and the light were discarded. The blanks were then flattened in batches in a form of vice, blanched, and marked on their edges using Blondeau's machine – such was the fear of counterfeiters, those who operated it were required to swear an oath of secrecy, although such machines were readily to be seen in Paris. Finally the blanks were coined (**11.9**). Let Samuel Pepys describe the scene:

> The Mill is after this manner; one of the dyes, which hath one side of the piece cut, is fastened to a thing fixed below; and the other dye (they tell me a pair of dyes will last the marking of 10000 l. before it be worn out, they and all other tools being made of hardened steel ...) to an engine above, which is movable by a screw which is pulled by men; and then a piece being clapped by one sitting below between the two dyes, when they meet the impression is set; and then the man with his finger strikes off the piece and claps another on; ... and then another and another, with great speed.
>
> (19 May 1663)

Fig. 11.10 Charles II, Tower shilling, 1674, milled coinage. The reappearance of Welsh feathers on some of the coins from 1671 onwards refers to silver sent to the Mint by the company of 'Undertakers for the working of Mines Royal in the counties of Cardigan and Merioneth', which began operations in 1670.

The work was exhausting and for some, hazardous; many moneyers lost one or more finger joints. It was also more expensive than the old way, but speedier and yielded a product that was neater, more consistent, and harder to clip or counterfeit. The coinage had begun to take on the appearance with which we remain familiar today (**11.10**).

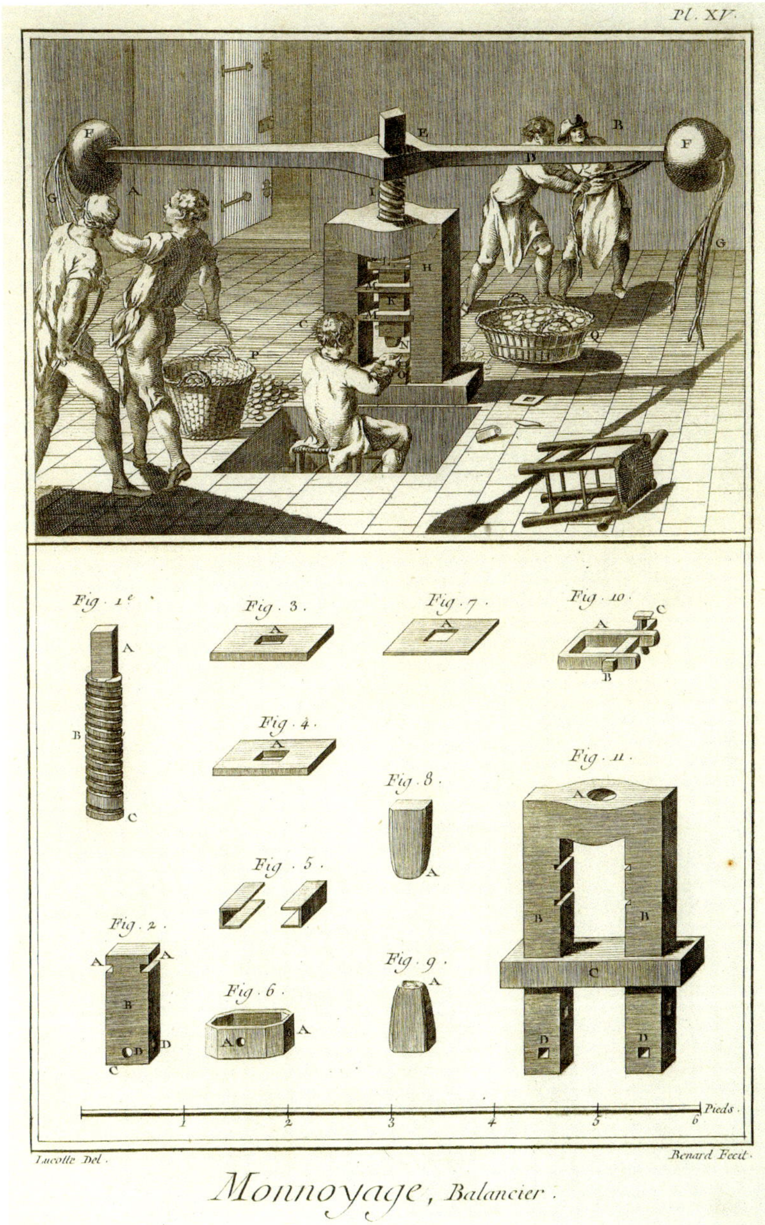

Fig. 11.9 The screw press in action, from Diderot and D'Alembert's *Encyclopédie*, 1771. This characteristic coining machine of the seventeenth and eighteenth centuries could produce up to 30 coins per minute and was only superseded when steam powered machines were introduced at the end of the eighteenth century. *National Museum of Wales, Library*

Postscript

What happened to the former Royalist mint masters? All survived the war and went through a very difficult decade before the new King's return saw them variously compensated for their sacrifices. Sir William Parkhurst, as we have seen, regained his former post of Warden of the Tower Mint, which he held until his death in December 1666. His colleague Thomas Bushell had his right to operate a mint confirmed by Oliver Cromwell and by Richard Cromwell, but it was never again exercised; Bushell pursued various mining projects, but none came to anything (**11.11**). In debt, as ever, he had every reason to maintain a low profile, especially when the hoped-for compensation of £36,000 he claimed to have spent on Charles I's behalf failed to materialise. The loss by fire of account books, etc. in his former Bristol lodgings on 17 February 1648 cannot have helped. He received only £1,000 of the £3,000 which was finally authorized in 1663. He died in April 1674 in a grace-and-favour apartment in Scotland Yard, part of the Palace of Whitehall.

Fig. 11.11 Thomas Bushell, copper-gilt mining token or share-ticket, *c.*1653. The obverse depicts Bushell's former patron, Sir Francis Bacon. The legend of the reverse translates as 'It is God who reveals what is shut away'.

Of the provincial masters, Cary, if we have identified him correctly, may have been the Sir Thomas 'Carey' who petitioned the Committee for Compounding in 1653 after having 'lost many thousands in Ireland by the late rebellion' and may therefore also have been the same Sir Thomas Cary Kt of Portlester, Co. Meath, whose Will was proved in the Prerogative Court of Ireland in 1662.

The Marquess of Newcastle, like many senior royalists, spent the interregnal years in exile, in Antwerp. At the Restoration, he returned to rebuild his shattered estates and to employ his leisure in literature (he wrote poems and plays) and horsemanship, the study and practice of which had led him to publish a major treatise in Antwerp in 1657. He was created Duke of Newcastle on 16 March 1665 and died on Christmas day 1676. His day-to-day master, William Martin, was denounced to the Committee for the Advance of Money on 23 May 1650; he was admitted to composition on 27 September and on 15 October was fined £83, or one-third of his personal estate – this high proportion (one-sixth or, if lucky, one-tenth were more normal) suggests strongly that Martin had played an active role in the 1648 risings. The will of a William Martin 'of the Citie of York Gentleman' was proved at Westminster on 30 November 1654.

Ormonde served Charles II in exile in France and was rewarded in due course with many honours, including a dukedom. As Lord High Steward of England, he carried the crown at Charles II's coronation. In 1661 he was again made Lord Lieutenant of Ireland, dismissed reluctantly by Charles in 1669, but reappointed from 1677 to 1685, dying in 1688.

Sir Richard Vyvyan, too, survived to witness the Restoration. His reward was to be made a gentleman of the Privy Chamber and Captain of St Mawes Castle, a Henrician coastal fort which, with Pendennis, guards the approaches to Falmouth and Penryn. The post, which members of his family had held in the past, carried the rank of Captain in the army and a salary of £182 *per annum*. These, and his baronetcy, were his recompense for the royalism that he calculated had cost him at least £10,000. He was MP for St Mawes from 17 March 1662 until his death on 3 October 1665 and is buried, with a simple memorial, in the church of St Mawgan-in-Meneage, near Trelowarren (**11.12**).

Fig. 11.12 Vyvyan's memorial, St Mawgan Church, Helston, Cornwall. *E Besly*

Royalist issues have necessarily attracted most attention in this survey. Their variety, their links with Charles, King and Martyr, their personal stories and the still unanswered questions associated with them have ensured this pre-eminence ever since they first received scholarly notice during the eighteenth century. The study of hoards and the few surviving output figures suggest, however, that they never accounted for more than a few per cent of the money available at the time, except for the occasional batch fresh from the mint, as at Pocklington, near York, where new half crowns from that mint may have formed one-third or more of a hoard found in 1848. Indeed, the Earl of Clarendon, royalist historian of the war, described the Shrewsbury mint as 'more for reputation than use'. Past collectors have ensured the disproportionate survival of royalist coins, removed as rarities from the many finds of the eighteenth and nineteenth centuries, the Tower Mint content of which then disappeared into the melting pot, its value (as in the 1640s) no more than that of its intrinsic silver content. We also owe the survival of the large gold pieces and the smallest silver coins, which were rarely hoarded, to the growth of the coin-collecting habit from the seventeenth century onwards. (Much coinage of the Commonwealth has no doubt survived for the same reason.)

Nevertheless, as we have seen, the royalist mints played a useful (sometimes vital) role at a local level. Their products, legitimate coins of the realm, continued to circulate down to the Great Recoinage of 1696, when all available hammered silver money was finally converted into new machine-made coinage (**11.13**); 'broad' gold lingered on until 1733. While the Tower Mint provided the bulk of the money handled by soldier and civilian alike, the royalist and other coinages described here give a variety and interest to the currency of England and Wales unmatched at any other time.

Fig. 11.13 Bristol half crown 1644 and Oxford shilling, 1643. The first survived intact until the Great Recoinage and in 1696 was officially punched through its middle to indicate a coin of full weight temporarily allowed to remain in circulation; the shilling, from a hoard found in 1984 near Builth Wells, Powys, succumbed to the drastic clipping which took place following a government promise to redeem clipped coin for recoinage at full face value.

APPENDIX 1

Sir Richard Vyvyan's Mint Commission, 3 January 1644

Charles by the grace of God King of England Scotland France and Ireland defender of the faith **To our trustie** and welbeloved Sir Richard Vivian knight greeting **whereas** our present affaires require the imployment of a mynt within our countyes of Devon and Cornwall And Cittie of Exon, **Knowe ye** that wee reposing speciall trust and confidence in your wise-dome skill abilities and care in and for that service doe hereby give you full power and authoritie by your selfe or your sufficient Deputy or Deputyes to erect and sett upp or cause to be erected and sett up one or more mynt or myntes in such place or places within our said countyes of Devon and Cornewall and Cittie of Exon or in any or either of them as you shall thinke fitt, and to make and engrave or cause to be made and engraven Irons and Stampes with our Effigies Inscriptions and Armes according to our present moneys in our Tower of London, and therewith to instamp and imprint or Cause to be instamped and imprinted all such Ingotts Bullion and plate of Gold or Silver as shalbe from tyme to tyme brought and delivered unto you or to any such mynt or mynts by any of our Subjects. And the moneys soe made and stamped to be of the same species weight and goodnesse as our foresaid moneys in our said Tower of London are and ought to be **and wee** doe further by theis present give full power and authoritie to you the said Sir Richard Vyvyan to doe in manner aforesaid all and every such thing and things in touching and concerning the premisses, as fully largely and amplie to all intents and purposes as the Officers or our mynt in our said Tower of London lawfully may do with Ingotts Bullyon or Plate brought to the mint there to be coyned, **and wee** doe hereby authorize you the said Sir Richard Vyvyan to receive for your paynes and charges in coyning all such Ingotts Bullion and Plate to be soe brought as aforesaid, the same allow-ances as in our said Tower are paid, and noe more, without any accompt to be rendered for the same **and our further** will and pleasure is and we doe hereby will and require you the said Sir Richard Vyvyan to pay or cause to be paid, soe much of the said moneys as shalbe made of all such Ingott Bullyon or Plate as shalbe delivered unto you or your said Deputyes, (or at the said mynt or mynts soe to be erected) by any of our subjects to our use unto our trustie and welbeloved Sir John Berkley Knight or such other person or persons as wee shall appoint, hee or they giving unto you upon every such payment a Note of Receipt under his or their hand for soe much money as shalbe paid. Which Note or Notes shall be to you a sufficient discharge against us our heires and Successors in that behalf **and our** will and pleasure is that theis our letters patent shall have continuance during our pleasure. **In witness** whereof we have caused theis our letters to be made patent **witnes** our selfe att Oxford the third day of January in the Nyneteenth year of our raigne

Per breve de privato Sigillo

Willys

APPENDIX 2: HOARDS AND HOARDERS

The decade of the Civil War has yielded an enormous quantity of unrecovered coin hoards; a small number of deposits of plate (silver spoons or vessels) have also been linked to the war. There were many reasons for depositing one's portable wealth securely at the time: forced or voluntary absence from home as men joined the armies; levies such as the Excise and local taxes ('contributions'), introduced as both sides desperately sought money; and anyone might be looted. Later in the 1640s came retribution as royalists were forced to compound for what was termed their 'delinquency', paying fines usually set at a sixth of their estates, occasionally if lucky only one-tenth. Sir Richard Vyvyan, royalist mint-master and soldier, was fined at one-tenth, indemnified under the Articles of Surrender of Exeter and with the support of Sir Thomas Fairfax, no less; and as we saw above in the case of William Martin, those who bore arms again in 1648 were hammered to the tune of one-third of their estates. Two of the very biggest hoards were buried in or after 1647: Middleham (N Yorks) and East Worlington (Devon): see below; and Tregwynt is at £51 9s 0d the largest hoard from Wales. If sequestration ('compounding') were not enough, the Commonwealth made a determined effort in the early 1650s to get its hands on unpaid taxes and other monies thought to have been raised in the royalist cause.

A small number of accounts of contemporary recovery have come down to us, such as Sir Henry Slingsby's gold and the hoard discovered at Halton Castle in 1658 (p.1). In 1643, royalist defenders of Wardour Castle, Wiltshire concealed £1,200 in money, plate and jewels before the castle was surrendered by Blanche, Lady Arundel. Col. Edmund Ludlow, commander of the Parliamentary garrison discovered it, when he in turn was besieged; part he used, but when he had to yield in March 1644, he and a servant reburied the remainder, revealing its whereabouts to Arundel's son after the war, as a return for the considerate treatment he had received after surrendering.

Tales of buried wealth fuelled a small boom in treasure hunting under the Commonwealth and after the Restoration. Down the years, there has been a steady stream of recovery. In March 1733 Sir Simon Stuart located a potful of coins in a field near his house at Hartley Mauditt, Hampshire, with the aid of a memorandum found amongst old papers and said to have been concealed by his grandfather Sir Nicholas Stuart, Bt 'in the time of the late Civil Wars'. Not long after, around January 1738, a poor boy named Thomas Love found 614 pieces of 'broad gold' in a coppice at Tunstall in Kent, said to have been buried by the royalist Sir Edward Hales, Bt. Newspapers of the eighteenth and nineteenth centuries carried accounts of the recovery of such hoards and thanks to the meticulous work of C. Stephen Briggs in searching digitised records, we now know numerous instances of hoards discovered during repairs to or demolition of older buildings (particularly as old thatch needed to be replaced) and through agricultural and infrastructure improvements. Farm workers and labourers came across hoards in the course of their work, grubbing out hedges and banks as well as during cultivation; navvies too, building the railways (Pocklington, 1848; Shipley, Derbyshire, 1890). With the patchy application of treasure trove procedures during the nineteenth century, such finds might come to official notice only after a cheerful evening in the local pub, as enjoyed by the fortunate 'ironstone getters' of Wingerworth, Derbyshire in 1856. Many coins were disposed to local silversmiths as 'old silver' at rates such as 4s 6d (Gloucester, 1847) or 5s 3d (Wingerworth); gold twenty-shillings of Charles I were valued at £1 0s 10d each in 1804 (Bolam, Northumberland). Other infrastructure works have played their part: the provision of main drainage for the village of Lazenby, Cleveland in 1879 finds a modern parallel in trenching for storm sewers in Wolverhampton (1999); both led to the finding of Civil-War hoards. Several hoards came to light in the nineteenth century as graves were dug in local churchyards; another in 1905 as a grave was prepared for a horse at Newsam Green, Leeds, at about the centre of a triangle formed by three 'ancient oaks'. Children (e.g., Foscote, Bucks, 1955) and animals have all played their parts: cows

(Muckleford, Dorset, 1935; Lutton, Northants, 1961), rabbits (Ashdon, Essex, 1984) and a mole (Wortwell, Norfolk, 1989).

In at least two cases local treasure legends have proved to have some basis in fact: Tregwynt (p.2) and East Worlington, Devon, where a tradition was handed down for generations of money concealed by a family named Cobley on a local farm; in 1895 workmen repairing a hedge bank brought to light three earthen vessels which between them contained 5,188 silver coins, amounting to £242 18s 10½d – numerically still the largest reliably-recorded Civil War hoard, though its value has since been overtaken by the £313 7s 3d found at Middleham (p.2).

Hoards unrecovered by their owners continue to be found at a steady rate, over 360 years later. Recovery peaked in the mid-nineteenth century and has fluctuated since, dropping during the two decades of world wars and rising in the decades of reconstruction and development that followed. Since around 1970, the advent of the metal detector has seen the rate rise again to around two per year, of every size from the small pursefuls lost away from habitations to the biggest of the lot, at Middleham.

The author and Stephen Briggs have jointly published an inventory comprising 347 hoards from the period 1625-1660, known to them at the end of 2012 (**Map 4**), but the finding goes on: among more recent finds is a small hoard from near Mold, Flintshire (2013), which included a 'Chester' half crown similar to **6.5**. Another hoard has also been found at Staveley, near Harrogate; closing in 1643-4, this includes a York half crown, a ducaton and three half-ducatons. Both conform to what are emerging 'regional' compositions. But does the dating and distribution of the Civil-War hoards reflect what was going on during the war? It used to be held that, other than forming a symptom of a time of crisis, the hoards did not 'follow the action'; however, with much more information now to hand, the evidence as it stands does show some apparent correlation. Of course, hoards can only be dated approximately, according to their latest coins, but with sufficient numbers, trends do become apparent. There are numerous Yorkshire hoards of 1643-4, but none closing in 1645, after Marston Moor (2 July 1644) effectively ended the war in the north; however, hoards closing 1646 or later put the county back on the map, perhaps because of the fighting there in 1648. The majority of south-eastern hoards likewise are 'late': the only serious fighting in the area took place in Kent and Essex in 1648; the Tregwynt hoard must surely be linked to the Pembrokeshire uprising of that year, too. Linking hoards to specific events is altogether harder, but the following may perhaps be suggested. The royalist (strictly, anti-parliamentarian) rebellion at King's Lynn in August 1643 – about the only actual fighting to take place in Norfolk – provides a likely occasion for the burial of a hoard of that year at nearby Dersingham, unearthed during building works in 1984; and the non-recovery of a hoard of 1644-5 from a basement in the Market Place at Leicester (found in December 1937) may perhaps be linked to Prince Rupert's sack of the town on 30 May 1645. The Tockwith hoard (terminus 1641-3, found in 2005) was likely lost on the battlefield of Marston Moor (2 July 1644) and the 1991 Sibbertoft find (1644-5) lay within 1,500 m of the centre of the Naseby battle (14 June 1645).

Hoards turn up almost anywhere, but particularly in or around buildings: under the floor, upstairs or down; under the hearth; in the basement; behind the skirting; in the wall; up the chimney; in the roof. This is inevitable in urban contexts, though the occasional hoard was buried in the yard or garden. A hoard amounting to £35 7s 9d in gold was found in 1874 by workmen demolishing buildings in the Old Court of Pembroke College, Cambridge; it is paralleled neatly by Sir Henry Slingsby's '£40 in gold'. The hiding place of choice for country people of modest means appears to have been the roof; those of greater means tended to use outbuildings/barns or their gardens, while one hoard was hidden beneath the capstone of a well at Allington in Wiltshire (October 1925). Quite a few hoards have been found in or near farms; those from Breckenbrough, North Yorkshire and Ampney St Mary, Gloucestershire (November 1935), were both bur-

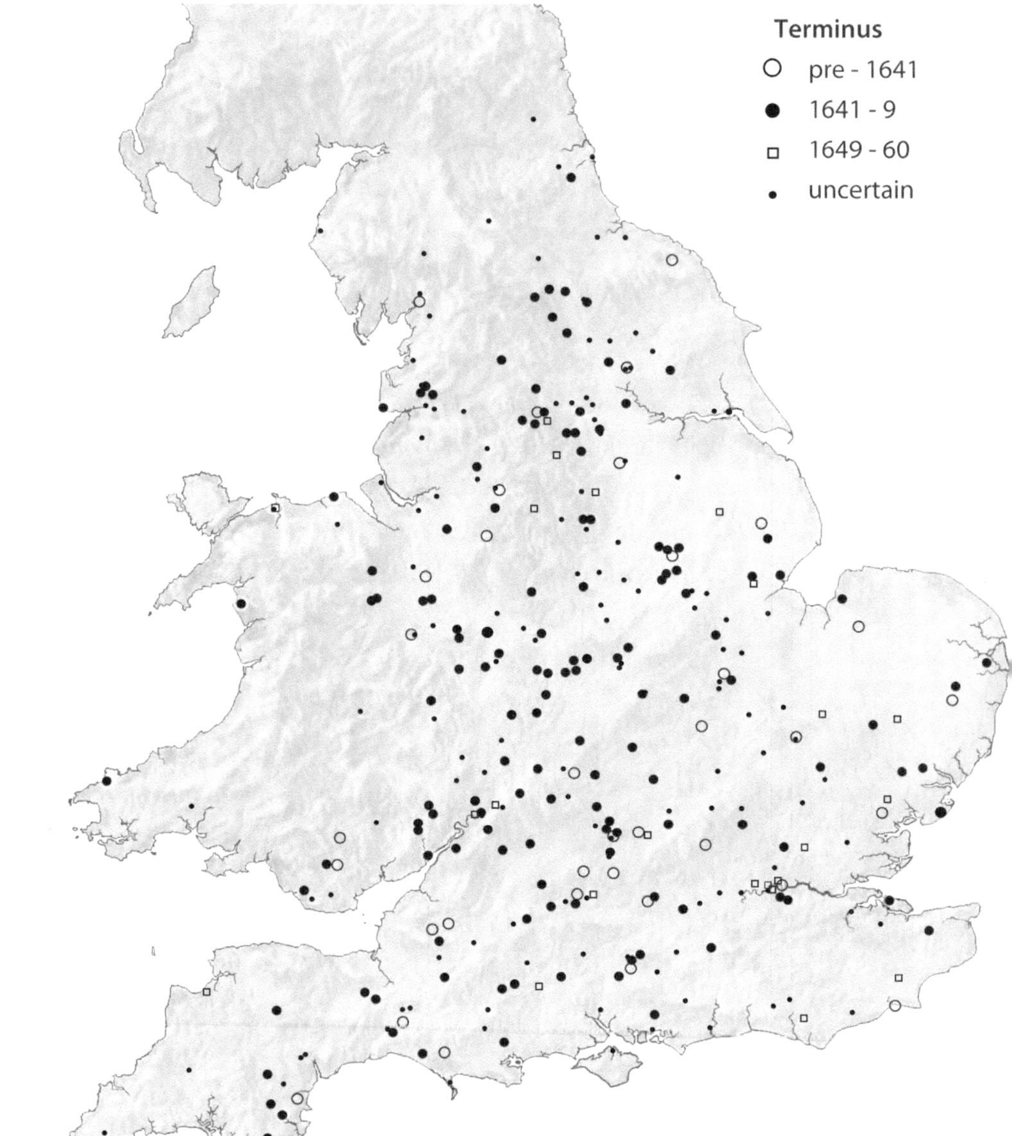

Map 4 England and Wales: hoards terminating 1625 – 1660. *Tony Daly*

ied just inside a farmyard wall and marked by large stones. The ruins of Fountains Abbey, near Ripon in North Yorkshire protected a hoard of silver coins buried in 1643-4, discovered during excavation of the monks' dormitory in 1850. Today, home improvements (Castle Cary, 2006), barn conversions (Prestbury, Cheshire, 2004) and garden groundworks (Tregwynt, 1996; High Ackworth, Wakefield, 2011) continue to yield hoards from the Civil War. The 1981 Weston-sub-Edge, Gloucestershire, hoard was buried in 1643 in the precise centre of a barn, latterly the village hall.

Away from buildings, hoards have been concealed in banks and lynchets, walls, the roots of trees (perhaps planted or used as markers?), in woodland or coppice and in stream and river banks. Boundaries might form significant markers: in June 1867 a boy found a hoard of 280 silver coins under the 'stem' of an oak tree, recently cut in Lovers' Coppice, on a bank which divided the parishes of Aldbourne and Ramsbury in Wiltshire ('Crowood').

Hoards vary in size from a few shillings to several hundred pounds – at the top end, comparable in today's terms to several hundred thousand pounds. It would appear that everyone was at it, from the meanest to the richest. We have already encountered several of the latter, but in broad terms the sizes and numbers of hoards parallel the sums of money recorded in contemporary and near-contemporary probate inventories, from the artisan to the gentleman; two-thirds of the hoards are sums of less than £10. Henry Kellway, gentleman, died in 1630 with £80 money in his possession and Samuel Fry, fisherman (1628), £1 13s 3d (both from Dorset); John Taverner, husbandman (Writtle, Essex, 1639), £11 14s 0d and Walter Parmiter, yeoman and carpenter (Dorset, 1627), £1 6s 4d. Widows such as Marie Lees (Lichfield, 1643: £31 14s 6d) and Elizabeth Toope (Dorset, 1640: 38 0s 0d) held much of their assets in ready money. For most people, portable wealth comprised current silver coin; at any one time each town or village will have held many such 'hoards', which when occasion demanded might be hidden securely, usually very close to home.

FURTHER READING

The list that follows can only scratch the surface of the huge literature of the English Civil War, both historical and numismatic – there are many excellent local and regional studies, for instance, the relevance of which will vary from reader to reader.

The Civil War and background

Barratt, J 2004	*Cavalier Generals: King Charles I and his commanders in the English Civil War 1642-1646*. Barnsley.
Bennett, M. 1997	*The Civil Wars In Britain & Ireland 1638-1651*. Oxford.
(Best, H.) 1857	The Account book of Henry Best, of Elmswell. [1616-44] *Rural Economy in Yorkshire*. Surtees Society 33, 149-64.
Brushfield, T.N. 1901	The financial diary of a citizen of Exeter, 1631-43, *Report and Transactions of the Devonshire Association*, 33, 187-269.
Chadwick-Healey, C.E.H. (ed.), 1902	*Bellum Civile: Hopton's narrative of his campaign in the West (1642-1644)*. Somerset Record Society XVIII.
Davies, G. 1959	*The Early Stuarts 1603-1660*. Oxford History of England, IX, 2nd Edition.
Duffy, C. 1979.	*Siege Warfare*. London. [Chapter 6: The English Civil War and the subjugation of Ireland.]
Engberg, J. 1966	Royalist finances during the English Civil War, *Scandinavian Economic History Review* XIV, 73-96.
(Eyre, A.) 1875	*A Dyurnall of catalogue of all my accions and expences from the 1st of January 1646*. Surtees Society 65. [Diary of a South Yorkshire yeoman, Adam Eyre.]
Firth, C.H. 1917	Sir Hugh Chomley's narrative of the Siege of Scarborough, 1644-5, *English Historical Review* 32, 568-87.

Gardner, S.R. 1886-91 *A History of the Great Civil War, 1642-1649*. 3 vols, London 1886-91; reissued in 4 vols, 1891. Reprinted, Windrush 1987.

Gaunt, P. 1991 *A Nation under Siege: The Civil War in Wales 1642-48*. London.

Gough, J.G. 1932 *The Superlative Prodigall: a life of Thomas Bushell*. Bristol.

Harrington, P. 2004 *English Civil War Archaeology*. London.

Holmes, C. 1974 *The Eastern Association in the English Civil War*. Cambridge.

Hutton, R. 1982 *The Royalist War Effort, 1642-1646*. London.

Jefferson, S. (ed.) 1840 *A Narrative of the Siege of Carlisle in 1644 and 1645 by Isaac Tullie*. Carlisle.

Millar, O. 1972 *The Age of Charles I: painting in England 1620-49*. London.

Ollard, R. 1976 *This War Without an Enemy*. London. [Well-illustrated general account.]

Parsons, D. (ed.) 1836 *The Diary of Sir Henry Slingsby, of Scriven, Bart*. London. [Includes an informative Civil War narrative of events in Yorkshire and elsewhere, and extracts from household accounts.]

Porter, S. 2011 *The Blast of War: destruction in the English civil wars*. Stroud.

Rogers, M. 1983 *William Dobson 1611-46*. London. [Catalogue of National Portrait Gallery exhibition; many royalist portraits.]

Wedgwood, C.V. 1955 *The King's Peace, 1637-1641*. London.

Wedgwood, C.V. 1958 *The King's War, 1641-1647*. London.

Numismatic and related works

For a detailed bibliography to 1983, see North and Preston-Morley, 1984.

Allen, D.F. 1940 The 'Weymouth' and 'Salisbury' mints of Charles I, *British Numismatic Journal* [*BNJ*] 23, 97-118.

Archibald, M.M. and Cowell, M.R. (eds) 1993. *Metallurgy in Numismatics, Volume 3*. London.

Barclay, C. 1994, A Civil War hoard from Middleham, North Yorkshire, *BNJ* 64, 84-96.

Bateson, D. 2007 The Castlecary hoard and the Civil War currency of Scotland, *BNJ* 77, 226-45. [A useful parallel survey. (Castlecary, near Falkirk)]

Berry, G. 1988 *Seventeenth Century England: traders and their tokens*. London.

Besly, E. 1984 The York Mint of Charles I, *BNJ* 54, 210-41. [See also *BNJ* 61 (1991), 129-32.]

Besly, E. 1987 *English Civil War Coin Hoards*. British Museum Occasional Paper 51, London.

Besly, E. 1991 'To reward their deservings': the badge for the Forlorn Hope, *The Medal* No.19, 21-7.

Besly, E. 1992 The English Civil War Mints at Truro and Exeter, 1642-1646, *BNJ* 62, 102-53.

Besly, E. 1993 Rotary Coining in Britain, in Archibald and Cowell 1993, 118-29.

Besly, E. 1998 A Civil War hoard from Tregwynt, Pembrokeshire, *BNJ* 68, 119-36.

Besly, E. 2015 Mapping conflict: coin hoards of the English Civil War, in Naylor, J. and Bland, R. (eds) *Hoarding and the Deposition of Metalwork from the Bronze Age to the 20th century: a British Perspective*, BAR British Series 615, Oxford, pp. 181-200.

Besly, E. and Briggs, C.S. 2013 Coin hoards of Charles I and the Commonwealth of England, 1625-60, from England and Wales, *BNJ* 83, 166-206.

Besly, E. and Cowell, M.R. 1991 The metrology of the English Civil War coinages of Charles I, *BNJ* 61, 57-75.

Boon, G.C. 1981 *Cardiganshire Silver and the Aberystwyth Mint in Peace and War*. Cardiff. [With reprints of Bushell's mining pamphlets and full bibliography.]

Boon, G.C. 1985 The Great Recoinage Hoard from Builth, *Archaeologia Cambrensis* 134, 210-24.

Brady, G. and Gallacher, C. 1986 — Munster "Siege Pieces" or early tokens?: evidence from a Cork scattering, *Spink's Numismatic Circular* [*NCirc*], April, 75-7.

Challis, C.E. (ed.) 1992 — *A New History of the Royal Mint*. Cambridge.

Coate, M. 1928 — The royalist mints of Truro and Exeter, 1642-6, *Numismatic Chronicle* [*NC*] 5th Ser. 8, 213-48.

Colgan, E. 2003 — *For Want of Good Money: the story of Ireland's coinage*. Bray, Co. Wicklow. [Chapter 11: A Kingdom divided.]

Cooper, D.R. 1988 — *The Art and Craft of Coinmaking: a history of minting technology*. London.

Dowle, A. and Finn, P. 1969 — *The Guide Book to the Coinage of Ireland, from 995 A.D. to the present day*. London.

Everson, T. 2007 — *The Galata Guide to The Farthing Tokens of James I & Charles I*. Llanfyllin.

Farquhar, H. 1914 — Nicholas Briot and the Civil War, *NC* 4th Ser. 14, 169-235.

Farquhar, H. 1928 — A lost coinage in the Channel Islands, *NC* 5th Ser. 8, 199-212.

Hawkins, E. 1885 — *Medallic Illustrations of the History of Great Britain and Ireland to the death of George II*. London. [Edited by A.L. Franks and H.A. Grueber; has few actual images. A companion edition, fully illustrated but with edited text, was published in parts, 1904-11 and reprinted (Seaby, London) in 1979.]

Jessop, H.R. 1976 — Flans for Newark Siege Coins, *NCirc*, March, 90-1.

Jones, M. 1979 — *The Art of the Medal*. London. [Chapter 8, pp.65-74, deals with English medals before 1660.]

Lessen, M. 1981 — The Cromwell Dunbar medals by Simon, *BNJ* 51, 112-33.

Lessen, M. 1997 — The Commonwealth naval medals for 1653, by Simon', *BNJ* 67, 48-72.

Lyall, R. 1971 — The Chester mint and the coins attributed to that mint, *NCirc*, March, 98-9.

Manville, H. 1982 — 'Caroli fortuna resurgam' siege pieces, *NCirc*, September, 229-32.

Nathanson, A.J. 1975	*Thomas Simon. His Life and Work 1618-1665*, London.
North, J.J. 1975	*English Hammered Coinage, Vol. II: Edward I to Charles II, 1272-1662*, 2nd Edition. London.
North, J.J. and Preston-Morley, P.M. 1984.	*Sylloge of Coins of the British Isles 33: the John G. Brooker Collection, Coins of Charles I*. London. [Includes essays on the Tower Mint (by J.P.C. Kent) and Civil War issues (G.C. Boon) and a comprehensive numismatic bibliography to 1983.]
Oman, C. 1934	A note on the coining of the royal plate at Newark in the year 1646, *NC* 5th Ser. 14, 74-80.
Platt, J.J. and Platt, A.K. 2013.	*The English Civil Wars: Medals, Historical Commentary & Personalities*. London.
Sellwood, D. 1986	The trial of Nicholas Briot, *BNJ* 56, 108-23. [English translation of a report of a trial of Briot's coining methods in Paris in 1617.]
Sharp, M.B. 1977	The Tower shillings of Charles I and their influence on the Aberystwyth issue, *BNJ* 47, 102-13.
Spink & Son Ltd 2015	*Coins of Scotland, Ireland and the Islands, Pre-decimal issues*, 3rd Edition. London.
Spink & Son Ltd 2018	*Coins of England and the United Kingdom, Pre-decimal issues*. London (new edition annually).
Symonds, H. 1910	Charles I; the trials of the pyx, the mint-marks and the mint accounts, *NC* 4th Ser. 10, 388-97.
Wright, G. 2002	The Civil War siege coinage, in Roberts, I., *Pontefract Castle. Archaeological Excavations 1982-86*. Yorkshire Archaeology 8, 282-7.

INDEX

Notes: All references are to pages. Hoards and finds have been indexed selectively.